NOTES FROM A NON-PROFITABLE LIFE

Martin C. Lehfeldt

With a Foreword by Steve Gunderson, President and CEO,
Council on Foundations

Editing, Design and Layout by WordPlay, LLC
Printed and published by Lulu.com
ISBN 978-0-557-02437-7

Dedicated to the memory of Joe Breiteneicher—
friend, mentor, and champion of the underdog.
As do all of us whose lives he touched, I miss him very much.

Table of Contents

Foreword

I first met Martin Lehfeldt when I became the President of the Council on Foundations, and he was still the President of the Southeastern Council of Foundations. He was introduced to me as an acknowledged leader within the ranks of the Forum of Regional Associations of Grantmakers. I soon recognized that candor (softened by humor) comes easily to Martin. More than candor, though, Martin brings a passion for and to the work of philanthropy by both public charities and grant makers.

It's my strong suspicion that the same gifts of communication and leadership that he demonstrated as the CEO of the Southeastern Council define his entire career of servant leadership on behalf of the non-profit sector (or the not-for-profit sector, as he prefers to call it). Four decades of engagement and collaboration, service, and leadership have provided him with a rich store of experiences from which he has distilled an equally meaty, although easily read, collection of observations.

The chapters about his time spent as a fund raiser and as a consultant to nonprofit organizations are laced with both wit and wisdom. His tributes to the importance of a generous spirit reflect deep though in each chapter. However, from my perspective as someone who spends his time working almost exclusively within the realm of foundations, I think the book reaches a wonderful crescendo during the final section about "organized" philanthropy. My favorite essay may well be "Committed to Change."

Why? Quite simply, a challenge philanthropy faces today is that of embracing transformation. Our sector is growing in both size and service, and yet we are also experiencing growing scrutiny from both the media and the policy makers. We need to move from competitive grant making to philanthropic leadership. Through accountability we must earn the confidence of those we seek to serve. Through advocacy we must engage in a level of communication that previously may have felt uncomfortable. Through change in our process, we seek greater impact in our work.

But all the change in the world holds no value unless we can transfer this opportunity for transformation to a new generation of philanthropy—those spurred by values to utilize their personal resources for public good and those motivated by professionalism to achieve new heights of service. In a very real sense, Martin's book is written for all of them. Each chapter pokes at the heart of the giver, while leaving a message of advice for those entering this noble work.

To all of you, enjoy this remarkable set of essays from a man who has done uncommon things in his work...and now in his writing.

Steve Gunderson
Alexandria, Virginia
October 4, 2008

Acknowledgements

This book is the product of relationships with hundreds of not-for-profit organizations and charitable foundations and experiences with literally thousands of their board and staff members. I am grateful to all of them.

As I was compiling these essays, some brave friends were willing to read various drafts of them. They offered sufficiently encouraging comments to keep me returning to the task of completing the book. I am indebted to (in alphabetical order) Joe Breiteneicher, Peter Brown, Bill Chace, Brenda Fiske, Barbara McInnis, Sam Pettway, Dot Ridings, David and Manuela Roosevelt, and Jamil Zainaldin for their cheerleading. Steve Gunderson, Sabrina Jones Niggel, Edward Queen, Betsey Russell, Manuela, and Jamil went further and volunteered not just encouragement but also detailed editorial commentary that improved the entire manuscript. Pattie Johnson at the Foundation Center Library in Atlanta supplied helpful research. Without Betsey Russell, a colleague of many years, who both provided editorial assistance and managed all of the production logistics, this book never would have been published. I apologize if I have omitted the names of others who helped me; it is a mark of creeping senility, not my ingratitude.

I've had only two bosses during my professional career. Both of these men had a great impact on my life. The first was Hans Rosenhaupt, President of the Woodrow Wilson National Fellowship Foundation in Princeton, and the other was Vivian W. Henderson, President of Clark College (now Clark Atlanta University). Many of the insights in this book are the direct result of their mentoring.

For the past 11 years, I have worked with several board chairs, and they too have taught me a great deal. So thanks, as well, to Larry I'Anson, former President of the Beazley Foundation; Russ Hardin, President of the Robert W. Woodruff Foundation; Frank Wideman, President of the Self Family Foundation; John Graham, a trustee of Baptist Community Ministries; Chip Gaylor, a trustee of the John and Patricia Buster Foundation; and Pete Bird, President of The Frist Foundation, as well as to all of the trustees of the Southeastern Council of Foundations who served during my tenure.

My thanks too to my predecessor, Robert Hull, and the SECF staff members, from all of whom I learned; the boards and staffs of our association's members; my many colleagues whose organizations constitute the Forum of Regional Associations of Grantmakers; and the members and staffs of the Council on Foundations, the Foundation Center, the Philanthropy Roundtable, and the Association of Small Foundations.

Finally, I am most appreciative to Linda, my wife of the past 19 years, who has patiently tolerated me working on these essays when I might have been spending time with her or contributing more to my share of household responsibilities.

Martin C. Lehfeldt
Atlanta, Georgia
October 2008

Introduction

I've spent my entire life working in or for the not-for-profit sector. For me it was never really a conscious choice. Whether the determining factor was nature or nurture remains open to debate. At any rate, I am a product of both the genetic material and the behavioral conditioning furnished by a minister father and a social worker mother. The notion of a career in the corporate world never occurred to me. After all, it took me quite a while to discover that the word "profit" wasn't spelled "p-r-o-p-h-e-t."

However, I obviously am more than the simple result of some mixture of biology and environment. Somewhere along the line I had to make my own choices about what I would do and why. The roots of the belief system that prompted my decisions are captured most powerfully in religious texts: the words of the Jewish prophets—figures like Isaiah and Amos, who insist that the only way to get right with God is to do justice—and the Jesus of the New Testament whose preaching calls for an end to all forms of oppression. During my lifetime, the Civil Rights Movement was one of the most significant responses to those pronouncements. When I hear someone like Georgia Congressman John Lewis recall Martin Luther King's simple phrase, "the beloved community," it speaks volumes to me.

The fact that I am the first member of my family to be born in this country also contributes to why I do what I do. Like many other children of immigrants, I believe strongly in that part of the American dream that includes the ideal of opportunity for everyone. In the final analysis, my career choices derive from the simple fact that I can't find anything else that gives me a greater sense of personal satisfaction.

At a very early age, my parents slipped a tape into my developing subconscious mind that essentially programmed me to follow the footsteps of my father and my grandfather into the Lutheran ministry. I never was able to erase it completely. During my senior year in college, as many classmates prepared their applications to graduate and professional institutions, I wanted more than anything else to go to the Columbia University School of Journalism. Instead, though, in 1961 I dutifully applied to Union Theological Seminary in New York City, was accepted, and faithfully reported for duty as a first-year student across Broadway from my first-choice destination.

My father died before I finished seminary, and that freed me psychologically to consider other pursuits. I did complete my course of study and received the requisite degree in 1965 but chose not to be ordained. Of course, that decision to self-defrock left me virtually unemployable. Who the hell was looking for someone with degrees in English literature and theology? Unfortunately, my fantasy of spending some time as a short-order cook in a diner by day and working on the Great American Novel at night proved not to be an option either; by that time I was married, and my wife was pregnant with our first child.

Nonetheless, I managed to stumble into a real job. Call it blind luck; attribute it to the grace of God; describe it as *kismet*—whatever. Within months of my graduation, we were loading up a moving van and driving down to Princeton, New Jersey, where I became the Director of Internship Programs for the Woodrow Wilson National Fellowship Foundation. My assignment was to identify former Woodrow Wilson and Danforth Fellows who had reached the master's degree level and were interested in "stopping out" for a while before resuming their doctoral studies. I recruited them and then placed them on the faculties of historically African-American colleges and universities around the South. I guess you could say that we were a kind of academic arm of the Civil Rights Movement.

Four years later, in 1969, envious that my charges were having all the fun, I myself traveled to the South and became the Vice President for Development at Clark College, a member of the consortium of educational institutions called the Atlanta University Center. Although I initially intended this move to provide a brief cultural experience, I stayed there for 10 years, including three as Director of Development for the Center itself.

Then in 1979 I formed my own consulting practice, based in Atlanta. For several years I was typecast as that white guy who raised money for African-American institutions, and I did indeed consult with quite a few of them. Eventually my client base expanded and I assisted a wide variety of other local, regional, and national not-for-profit organizations with fund raising, planning, and organizational development. The business supported me and my family for 18 years.

In 1994 the Southeastern Council of Foundations (SECF) retained me to conduct an initiative designed to establish and strengthen community foundations throughout the region. Four years later, when my predecessor announced his plans to retire, I applied for and eventually was offered the presidency of SECF. I held that position for 11 years. My primary motivation for this career shift had little to do with the chance to direct the affairs of a membership organization. Rather, I was intrigued by the notion that the increasing number and collective assets of grant making foundations had the potential to make a significant difference in Southern life, and I wanted to help encourage that movement.

Several years ago, with the encouragement of colleagues, I began collecting some of my observations about the not-for-profit sector that I had composed for speeches and articles as well as adding to them. I didn't want to write a comprehensive analysis or history; a lot of thoughtful people already have contributed to a rich library of publications about the sector. Much of it, though, is insider information—written by practitioners for practitioners. If possible, I wanted to produce something that would be accessible not just to professionals but also to volunteers and other interested people.

I put together a collection of musings that roughly paralleled my personal career. However, even after I had assembled a series of essays about topics that struck me as either noteworthy or even important, something still seemed to be missing. Most of those who reviewed what I had produced declared it to be interesting and even enjoyable, but a couple of the readers kindly suggested that I needed to drill deeper— to couple my observations with some further interpretation and even counsel.

Even as I attempted to follow their advice, though, I still felt stymied. Finally, I turned for guidance to my friend Dr. Edward Queen, Director of the D. Abbott Turner Program in Ethics and Servant Leadership at

Emory University's Center for Ethics. Despite that weighty title, he is also one of my favorite drinking buddies. Perched on a bar stool at Manuel's Tavern, I explained my dilemma to him. He had already read the manuscript once and pronounced it to be satisfactory as a personal memoir. However, he also understood the interest in having the book offer what the current jargon sometimes describes as *gravitas*. He asked me a single question—one that I had never actually put to myself. "Why are you really writing this book?"

As best I can recall, I said something like "I think I've gained some insights about the not-for-profit sector that might be useful to both professionals and volunteers and perhaps even encourage young people and second-career folks to consider working in it. I also want the readers to understand that people who devote their lives to the not-for-profit sector are engaged in a high calling. It's not without its flaws, and we all need to be able to laugh at ourselves when we make mistakes, but what we are doing is essential for the preservation of democracy." For whatever reason, that reply suddenly opened the way to the completion of the pages that follow.

As you read the book, you'll discover that some themes appear with regularity. That's easy to explain with a concept I borrowed from P. C. Enniss, a former pastor of the church to which I belong: the older I get, the less certain I am about many matters, but the more convinced I am about those things that matter most to me.

DEMOCRACY'S GLUE

The United States is the wealthiest nation in the world. Everywhere one looks is evidence of what the engine of capitalism has produced. Our competitive, for-profit, market-driven economic system has encouraged spirited and productive entrepreneurship. American companies have developed life-saving and labor-saving products and produced a cornucopia of items that comfort, amuse, and delight. The entire system has also provided the opportunity for a large number of individuals to acquire significant assets.

However, our national identity involves much more than the generation of wealth. Hidden in plain view is another side of our character without which our society might well collapse. It is the not-for-profit sector. Once your powers of observation have been trained to see this society through a not-for-profit lens, it's impossible to walk down the main thoroughfare of any municipality without noticing the impact of charitable organizations. The museums and theaters, the libraries, the churches, the daycare centers, the social welfare agencies, the universities, and the hospitals all exist in no small measure because caring and generous individuals gave of their wealth and other resources to create and sustain them. According to *Giving USA 2008*, Americans in 2007 contributed $306,390,000,000 (that's right, more than $306 billion!) to support these important organizations. Nearly 80% of this money came from individuals and some 7% from bequests; another 12% was granted by foundations; and 5% from corporations. The total was almost four per cent higher than in the previous year.

The pattern of American citizens' sense of responsibility for each other has been going on for many years. One of the first to describe it was Alexis de Tocqueville, the French author of *Democracy in America*, who came to this country in 1831. Scarcely a day passes that his observations about American society are not quoted—or misquoted— by some politician or academic. Perhaps his most cited lines are that "Americans of all ages, all stations of life, and all types of disposition are forever forming associations....In democratic countries knowledge of how to combine is the mother of all other forms of knowledge; on its progress depends that of all the others."

Edward Queen, my aforementioned scholarly friend, shares my weariness with this citation and my desire for a new authority to reference. As he once wryly noted, "After all, the guy was just 25 years old when he visited America, and he only stayed for nine months."

If I were to try to update de Tocqueville, I might offer the following observation: "Americans are not unique in having a charitable impulse and the desire to help their neighbors. However, they have managed to organize a society whose government and tax laws actively encourage a free-standing sector of agencies and institutions whose broad purpose is to improve the well-being of all its citizens." One thing is clear: our long-standing mores of charitable giving and voluntarism constitute a truly amazing dynamic that I believe undergirds our democracy.

They also are having an international impact. We take pride in the fact that emerging market economies around the world have modeled themselves after American free enterprise. However, some self-congratulation may also be in order for the eager embrace of our not-for-profit systems by other nations. They too are realizing that for their new economies to work requires the corollary of a strong charitable sector. It is one of our great unsung exports. The next two essays are reflections on this sector.

What's in a Name?

Those who were privileged to know Paul Ylvisaker were blessed indeed. His distinguished career included service as a professor at Swarthmore, Princeton and Harvard, director of the Ford Foundation's public affairs program, chair of President Lyndon Johnson's Task Force on the Cities, Commissioner of Community Affairs for the State of New Jersey, Dean of the Harvard Graduate School of Education, Senior Consultant to the Council on Foundations, and board member of several foundations. For many of us he was the leading guru of the not-for-profit sector.

Dr. Ylvisaker was a font of insights and trenchant observations. One that stuck with me was a question he posed while addressing an annual meeting of what then was called the Atlanta Community Foundation. His remark was almost a throw-away line. "Why," he asked, "is the nonprofit field the only one that describes itself with a negative?" Why indeed? Can you think of any other positively oriented collection of people in our society who define themselves so self-disparagingly?

The more I've pondered his question, the more certain I am that the answer has to do with our economic values. We operate in a capitalistic society in which profit is the coin of the realm. Ours is also a society whose fiscal strength depends upon all of us shopping till we drop. Our motto is "Veni, Vidi, VISA." Yet we don't refer to consumers as non-savers, do we?

Now that we've moved from being an agrarian country to an industrialized and technologically driven nation, we don't describe factory workers and computer programmers pejoratively as non-farmers. How would those of you who don't work in educational institutions like to be referred to as non-thinkers? Similarly, I don't think academicians want to be called non-workers? Implied in the term "non-profit" is the notion of non-productivity —and clearly, nothing could be further from the truth.

Our society places enormous demands and expectations upon that vast network of approximately 1.4 million agencies and organizations that in turn rely upon an intricate array of public support, private contributions and millions of hours of voluntarism to sustain themselves. We ask and expect them to feed the hungry, clothe the naked, heal the sick, and, in the words of an old hymn, to rescue the perishing and care for the dying. They work hard to clean up the mess from our environmental pollution, to maintain educational institutions and systems, and to enhance the quality of our lives through art and music—and most of them do so with inadequate resources.

By the way, it is a myth that our nation's grant-making organizations could assume the financial burden of government to safeguard the education, health, and welfare of all Americans—especially those who are handicapped by discrimination and disability. If these foundations had liquidated their collective assets of some $580 billion in 2006, those funds would have provided less than 3 per cent of the following year's $2.8 trillion federal budget. Indeed, many of those not-for-profit organizations could not exist without significant public subsidy. However, despite their financial limitations, one can make the case that they are indeed the glue that holds together our democracy. They do so because they demonstrate the nature of true citizenship—a sense of responsibility for the well-being of our fellow creatures. Dr. Jamil Zainaldin, the President of the Georgia Humanities Council, puts it this way: "In an economic climate whose success depends upon all of us being consumers, the sector in which we labor is a continual safeguard against greedy self-absorption." Its members further provide a meaningful answer to the question, "What difference can one person make?" And yet we continue to relegate these organizations and agencies to second-class citizenship by labeling them with a negative name.

Far wiser minds than mine have wrestled with the challenge to come up with a better name. John Gardner, the former head of the Carnegie Corporation, became Secretary of Health, Education & Welfare during President Lyndon Johnson's administration and later was the principal architect and leader of the National Urban Coalition and Common Cause. He proposed that we call this voluntary network the "Independent Sector." However, that name never really took either, despite the fact that Gardner helped form the organization of the same name that continues in existence. "Third Sector" doesn't ring my chimes either, nor am I especially fond of phrases like "civil society."

It seems to me that what we're about, when we're at our best, is the building of community, but I haven't come up with the right phrase to capture that concept either. For the time being, we're stuck with this negative descriptor of our field. Maybe we can start a movement to re-name it. My only contribution thus far has been to go on periodic crusades to substitute "not-for-profit" for "nonprofit," as I have tried to do throughout this book.

My temporary solution at least proclaims intentionality on our part. It emphasizes that our motivation for doing what we do is *not* to increase our personal financial security. I invite you to join me in the search for a more positive tagline to describe the important work we have embraced. However, whether or not we are successful in re-christening ourselves, I have every confidence that the essential activity of the sector will continue and that our society will become ever stronger because of it.

Our Mutual Pledge

The ringing words of Thomas Jefferson that conclude the Declaration of Independence state: "...with a firm reliance on the protection of divine Providence, we mutually pledge to each other our Lives, our Fortunes and our sacred Honor."

To re-read that profound document is to be reminded that this assertion of the colony's autonomy was also the affirmation of a mutual bond of its citizens to each other. In addition to being an assertion of the right to self-rule, it was a declaration of interdependence.

Many Americans feel uncomfortable with the notion of interdependence. An old poem that some of us memorized when we were much younger is called, "Invictus." Its highlight is this proud pronouncement: "I am the captain of my fate, I am the master of my soul." Nothing better captures our highly vaunted spirit of rugged individualism.

I happen to think it's a crock. I don't believe that any of us is the captain of her fate or the master of his soul. Of course, all of us know individuals who claim to be self-made, and I've always been further intrigued by how many of them praise their creator daily. Frank Davis, Executive Director of The Cannon Foundation, is fond of describing some of them as folks who were born on third base but go through life thinking they hit a triple. They're kidding themselves. We all are products of our relationships with many other people and what they have done for us.

The signers of the Declaration of Independence, as old Ben Franklin put it, knew that if they didn't hang together, they would hang separately. Ironically, then, the individualism we all cherish rests ultimately upon a foundation of mutuality. Our economic system is a powerful engine for growth and development. Nonetheless, as I have already noted, the not-for-profit sector is the adhesive that holds us together and reminds us of our responsibility to each other. That may well be the heart of its greatness.

Robert Putnam has done a lot of research on this web of relationships.

The Peter and Isabel Malkin Professor of Public Policy at Harvard University wrote a seminal book called *Bowling Alone*—an exploration of the way in which people connect with and demonstrate a sense of responsibility for each other. He describes this fabric of networks as "social capital."

Social capital includes the formation of charitable institutions, the organization of Little Leagues and Girl Scout troops and Jack and Jill Clubs. It embraces building campaigns and the mobilization of blood drives and people helping each other after both natural and man-made disasters. It's a wonderful tradition—one that is hundreds of years old. During the early days of our country, we came together to raise barns and build places of worship. We helped each other to harvest our crops, and we organized agencies and mutual aid societies to help our neighbors in need. We serve on boards and join volunteer fire companies and help out in our local hospitals. We also have a tradition of financial generosity—making contributions to our churches and synagogues, to health agencies, to colleges and schools, to community chests, and to thousands of other helping organizations, as well as establishing foundation endowments.

Dr. James Joseph, former President of the Council on Foundations and former U. S. Ambassador to South Africa, has properly reminded us in his writings and speeches that the tradition is not unique to the United States. Today, as they have for thousands of years, citizens around the world continue to share their talents and skills for the well-being of their communities...and they have specific vocabulary to describe this phenomenon. Thus, for example, the Cherokee language uses the word *gadugi* to describe tribal members coming together as a community to assist each other.

Several years ago I had the privilege of helping to organize the Anguilla Community Foundation. While visiting that small Caribbean island, I learned that they delightfully describe their neighbor-helping-neighbor tradition as "jollification." (They also seem to be light-years ahead of us on the voluntarism front; when their citizens gather to repair someone's storm-damaged house or boat, the event includes the liberal dispensation of rum.)

As members of a community come together and pool their resources for the common good, all kinds of seemingly impossible things become possible. The outpouring of gifts and volunteer service in response to the horror that visited New York and Washington on September 11 is an example of this principle at work as is the willingness of people throughout the world to contribute to relief efforts after a terrible *tsunami* devastated the coastlines of Southeast Asia and Hurricanes Katrina and Rita hit our own shores.

Someone else has observed that another way of describing social capital is to note that it can be anything that causes people to talk about themselves as "we" and "us" instead of "I" and "them". The survival of all democratic societies depends upon the encouragement and demonstration of true citizenship—a sense of responsibility for our community; a commitment to making it a place in which no one is forgotten or left behind; or, as Mr. Jefferson put it, the pledging of our "Fortunes" to one another.

We often see these forces at work in our neighborhoods. In one sense, a neighborhood can closely resemble an extended family. Its members may not be especially close-knit; they certainly don't see eye-to-eye on every issue. Nonetheless, recognizing that they share a common space and the common desire for a safe environment in which to live, they engage in routine acts of civility. They know each others' names and speak to each other; they take in each other's mail and packages when requested; they borrow each other's tools; they admonish each other's misbehaving children; if they disagree about something, they try to do it respectfully. When the neighborhood's stability is endangered by, say, a proposed highway that will bisect the community or the disappearance of municipal services, they rally to combat the threat.

To be sure, a neighborhood is a much more complex organism than what I have described. My point simply is to highlight the importance of neighborliness as an important social value—one that should never be taken for granted and one, therefore, that is worthy of conscious attention, cultivation, and support.

I realize that some folks find all of this talk about communal activity to be cloying. They're suspicious about its potential to devalue personal liberty. However, I'm convinced that civic engagement and neighborliness don't have to stand in opposition to that cherished American ideal of individualism. Indeed, I would go so far as to contend that the value of self-expression is best safeguarded—as well as monitored—in a society that celebrates the richness of both neighborly differences and mutual concerns.

When Anna Faith Jones, the former CEO of The Boston Foundation, retired, the Council on Foundations honored her for her many contributions to the field of philanthropy. In her response, she said something that has stuck with me ever since. As we go about the work of grant making, she observed, "Democracy must be our first charity." Perhaps, in the final analysis, our not-for-profit sector is in the business of building a nation and a world of neighbors.

CHASING THE CHARITABLE DOLLAR

The not-for-profit sector sometimes seems to be roughly divided into two classes of people: those who have the discretionary financial resources to expend on charitable purposes and those who spend a great deal of their time looking for the keys to the vaults that hold this treasure. Put more simply, some people have money to contribute and the rest are doing their best to get a portion of it. It was my privilege to spend 10 years as a college development officer and another 18 as a consultant to organizations that depended upon fund raising to keep their organizations alive and well.

When the subject comes up, most people readily assert that they "hate fund raising." To their way of thinking, it's simply a higher order of panhandling. They're mistaken. The solicitation of contributions is all about sales. However, instead of selling a vacuum cleaner or a security service, you're offering prospective donors the opportunity to invest in something that will contribute to a stronger community and society. Those who resist making the "sales" call also fail to realize that the odds are on their side if they solicit someone they know; all the studies I've seen confirm that people are most likely to contribute if asked by a friend...especially if that friend has made his or her own financial commitment.

One school of thought holds that both paid employees and volunteers abhor fund raising because it carries with it the threat of rejection. My experience further suggests that this fear abates once they recognize that they don't have to take it personally. Instead they need to understand that those who decline their solicitations are simply— and unfortunately—missing out on the chance to invest in something important and even noble.

This section is not intended to be a fund raising manual, but I did want to share a few anecdotes and observations gleaned from my experiences of looking for the financial fuel to keep the not-for-profit engine running smoothly.

I'm Proud to Have Been a Fund Raiser

Fund raisers tend to get a bad rap. They're not the butt of quite so many jokes as lawyers, but…well, for example, it's been asserted that every fund raiser should have a pimp for an older brother so he or she will have someone to look up to.

The truth of the matter is that the fund raising profession has its share of slimeballs and nogoodniks, but then so do the priesthood and the ranks of corporate executives. I am proud to claim that I was once a card-carrying member of what then was called the National Society of Fund Raising Executives (now the Association of Fundraising Professionals). Putting my own theological spin on things, I regarded my work as a kind of ministry to the wealthy. By separating them from their treasure and providing them with opportunities to direct some of their money to worthwhile causes, I was offering them if not salvation at least a greater sense of personal well-being.

Virtually everything I know about fund raising, I learned from Irving Warner. I first met Irving when he came from California in 1963 to run a big campaign in New York for the Center for the Study of Democratic Institutions and hired my wife as his secretary. Some years later, after I started work at Clark College, the president and I decided that we needed to embark upon a major fund raising drive. I immediately called Irv for help. A short while later we retained his services as our campaign consultant.

Over the years, I introduced my own improvisations on what he taught me, but the essentials he imparted have served me well. He picked up his fund raising skills from his own mentors in the bare-knuckle fund raising rings of Israel Bonds and synagogue campaigns all over the United States and Canada. He's proud to be called a fund raiser and snorts with disdain at people who describe their work as institutional advancement or even development. He loves to show his clients how to ask for money. Don't even get him started on expressions like "friend raising"! So what did I learn from Irving? Enough to fill a book, but he already wrote it years ago. If you can find a copy of *The Art of Fund Raising*, you'll be rewarded by one of the more enjoyable introductions to the subject that you'll ever encounter.

One thing that always stuck with me was Irving's insistence on keeping things simple. He was fond of explaining that every fund raising campaign has four essential ingredients. He called them the four Cs: a case, a constituency, a chairperson and a committee. The case, of course, refers to the story you have to tell and tell well. Constituency is shorthand for making sure that you have a carefully defined audience to which you will tell your story. Chairperson translates into leadership with clout—without which, Irving asserts correctly, no fund raising campaign can succeed. (In his words, "If you don't have leadership, you've got *bupkis*.") It doesn't have to be a single person. On more than one occasion during my consulting days, when my clients couldn't find a strong campaign chair, we went with a team of strong individuals whose collective influence proved to be a reasonable alternative. Finally, committee is another way of describing the organization of the worker bees whose job it is to make the solicitations.

Irving has great appreciation for attractive promotional materials; he has organized enormous special events; he knows how to write a proposal to a foundation. But don't let him hear you say that any of those products or activities constitutes fund raising. Successful fund raising, he contends, occurs when the right solicitor asks the right prospect, face-to-face, for the right amount of money at the right time. Everything else is background music.

I think one of the greatest lessons I learned from him was the value of gift tables. People tend to forget that those fascinating little pyramids exist to document an essential point: fund raising is not an egalitarian enterprise. Some people have more money than their fellow human beings and, *ergo*, should be asked to give more. As the old truism puts it, a successful campaign is going to raise about 80 per cent of its goal from about 20 per cent of the contributors—and I have encountered precious few exceptions to that axiom. (A later chapter in this book describes one of them.)

Once you have grasped that concept, you never again will go after a prospective donor for $100 when she should be giving $1,000. During my 18 years as a consultant, I lost track of the number of clients who told me that they planned to raise, say, $100,000 by asking one thousand people each to give $100. Their computational skills were, of course, indisputable. One hundred times 1,000 does indeed equal 100,000. The problem was that they didn't know a thousand people who were likely to give them $100, and so, once again, we would develop a gift table.

The first successful campaign with which I was involved after I opened my own business was for a small not-for-profit organization in Atlanta that set out to raise approximately $400,000. That doesn't sound like much money these days, but 30 years ago, it was a king's ransom for a struggling operation with very few regular supporters and severely limited visibility. The good news was that one of its board members, the vice president of a major national corporation in the city, had successfully recruited his boss—the company's new CEO—to serve as chairman of the drive. Obviously, therefore, the corporation would have to make a pace-setting gift to the campaign. Whatever it pledged would set the tone for other contributors.

Since the agency had a rather small list of prospects, I worked very hard on a gift table and finally concluded that we could make our goal if the lead gifts came in at the right level. One of my employees who had been assigned to the campaign went off to discuss the gift from the chairman's company with the vice president who sat on the agency's board. He proudly returned with the news that we would receive a $40,000 gift and was crestfallen when I told him it wasn't enough.

I don't know where I got the courage to do it, but I told him that he'd have to go back and insist that the pledge be increased by $10,000. Otherwise, I asserted, the rest of the major givers would peg their contributions at a lower level, and the campaign would fail. To his credit, he delivered that very rude message, survived the angry response, and got the increased pledge. The other major gifts fell into line, and we made our goal.

A second lesson that has stood me in good stead is the need to appreciate the big distinction between a suspect and a prospect. A suspect is anyone with money; a prospect is someone with money to whom you have personal access. It's very easy to compose long lists of men and women whose wealth you would like to capture for the welfare of your not-for-profit organization. All too often, as I and my clients would begin planning campaigns, well-meaning but ill-informed friends would volunteer the names of wealthy individuals whose names frequently appeared in the press. The roster generally included film actors, professional athletes, corporate CEOs, entrepreneurs, and the heirs to great fortunes. Certainly it's a delicious feeling to fantasize that you could ask Paul Newman or the chairman of Exxon/Mobil for support. Unfortunately, our friends had no idea how to gain access to them. Compiling these kinds of lists is an exercise in futility if you don't have someone in your ranks who has a relationship with these high-profile folks and can approach them for contributions.

I also learned that there is an enormous difference between a constituency and a non-constituency campaign. If you're raising funds for a university or a church, virtually all of your prospects are going to be people with whom you have a connection—alumni, parishioners, and so on. On the other hand, if you're trying to solicit support for an alternative theater company or a struggling homeless shelter, you face a very different kind of challenge. When Notre Dame or the biggest Baptist church in town launch drives, much of their work is akin to a full-scale military invasion. The campaign for a not-for-profit organization with no significant constituents is more like guerrilla warfare in which you solicit selected prospects and build from one small success to the next.

Perhaps the most important insight Irving Warner shared with me was a citation from the Talmud. It essentially notes that anyone who makes a generous contribution is blessed, but that someone who persuades another person to be generous is doubly blessed. Good fund raisers, be they professionals or volunteers, are not beggars. Using a combination of skills, they are agents who help to promote increased generosity—one of the greatest human expressions of love, mercy and justice.

Getting Kissed Off in the Oak Room

You don't last long as a fund raiser if you can't deal with rejection. Of course, you're always working to reduce the odds of that happening—by carefully building relationships and doing everything else in your power to position the moment of requesting a contribution to be a positive experience. Nevertheless, "ask and you shall receive" is an admonition that doesn't always hold true; neither does that old bromide, "The money's out there; just ask for it." I've had my share of successes, but over the years I and my employers and clients have been turned down cold by any number of prospective donors.

I decided at some point that what really rubbed salt in the wound of these rejections, though, were the circumstances under which we were kissed off. Here's a true story from around 1972 when Clark College was in its first major capital campaign. Someone had made arrangements for the president, our fund raising consultant, and me to meet with a major gift prospect—a very busy man who insisted that the only time in his schedule when he was available would be over breakfast. He suggested that we meet him in the Oak Room at the Plaza Hotel in New York.

Those were the days early in my career when I was still easily impressed by the trappings of wealth, and the Plaza represented a style of living that was the stuff of dreams. The furnishings in the lobby, the liveried staff, the limousines parked at the curb were all reminders that I was out of my league when I entered this home-away-from-home for the rich and famous.

Nonetheless, our expensively garbed host with a shine on his shoes in which he could see his reflection was gracious and did a nice job of putting us at ease. A waiter arrived with the menus, and I almost choked when I saw the prices of the dishes being offered. Down the block and around the corner on Sixth Avenue, as I knew from personal experience, was a diner where the java cost a dime and you could get a great breakfast for less than three dollars. (Yes, it was a long time ago.) Here in the Oak Room, they were charging more than a buck for a cup of coffee and everything else was priced accordingly.

Having placed our orders, we then settled into a pleasant conversation, all of which led to the moment when we proposed to our prospective donor that he make a significant contribution to our campaign. Not to belabor the story, he then carefully explained that he already had too many other philanthropic commitments and would be unable to help us. That said, he picked up the meal tab for the four of us—it approximated the cost of my plane ticket from Atlanta—and bid us farewell. In retrospect, I would have preferred to forego the eggs Benedict I had enjoyed and instead received a check in the amount of the cost of breakfast.

For a while I kept a list of the most expensive places in which people have told me that they couldn't support the institution or cause for which I was trying to raise money. On that list was a very toney private club atop one of the highest buildings in San Francisco where someone else told the president and me—over an outrageously priced meal of fresh Dungeness crabs—that he couldn't help us. Another was an elegantly furnished office in a Chicago high rise where the owner of major perfume company listened to my associate and me make the pitch, declined to support us, and then concluded by saying, "You're a nice couple of guys; let me give you each a bottle of musk oil to take home with you." And that's exactly what he did.

What can I say? When you work in the part of the not-for-profit sector that's on the asking side of the equation, you are all too often reminded of the yawning chasm that seems sometimes to stretch between the "haves" and "have-nots." I long since stopped being annoyed about these experiences and can even laugh about them. Even so, though, I encourage those with the power to disburse charitable dollars to be sensitive to the precarious emotional state and financial security of those who come in search of support.

Hunting for Big Game

When I was hired to start Clark College's first development office back in 1969, the institution had no wealthy individual supporters. Of course we devoted a lot of time to cultivating new donors and strengthening alumni giving, but we also realized that we needed to build bridges to grant-making foundations.

We weren't on a first-name basis with any of their leaders, so, like many other institutions, we turned to *The Foundation Directory*—a thick volume that weighed several pounds. The experience of discovering this resource was not unlike that of someone wandering lost in the desert and suddenly spotting the glorious mirage of a lush oasis. Clark, like any struggling liberal arts college, had an entire catalogue of needs—for buildings, equipment, faculty salaries, scholarships, new programs. And here in this single volume was a list of hundreds upon hundreds of charitable institutions who existed precisely to address those kinds of needs. As I pored through its pages, I found what appeared to be a marriage truly made in heaven. To my still untutored way of thinking, the path was clear. I would send proposals to these foundations, and they would fund them.

Drawing upon all of my rhetorical skills, I began crafting beautifully written, persuasive, and even inspirational arguments for why those foundations should consider our college worthy of their generous support. I would then slap the requisite postage on the envelopes and commit them to the custody of the U.S. Post Office.

Weeks—often months—would pass before I received a reply. Finally, though, a letter bearing the return address of a foundation I had solicited would arrive in my mail box. With trembling fingers, hoping against hope, I would rip open the envelope and read this kind of message:

Dear Mr. Lehfeldt:

Thank you for your proposal. Unfortunately, our foundation receives more requests than its resources will permit it to support. Therefore, we must decline the opportunity to respond positively to your inquiry. Please be assured that our decision in no way reflects upon the merits of your proposal.

Sincerely yours,

I would re-read this formulaic missive, searching for clues—some nuance of language that might offer a glimmer of hope. Forget it. After receiving dozens of these kinds of epistles, I painfully learned how to translate what these letters really were telling me:

> Dear Mr. Lehfeldt:
>
> We got your proposal along with a bunch of other unsolicited pleas from organizations we don't know anything about. Nobody read it (unless one of the secretaries glanced at it before she threw it in the wastebasket). The only reason we're sending you this response is because we were raised to be polite. Besides, who needs bad PR these days.
>
> Sincerely yours,

That was back in 1969, when there were far fewer foundations than today. There soon will be more than 75,000 foundations in the United States—a number that seems to be increasing almost exponentially as the intergenerational transfer of wealth plays itself out. Thanks to technology, information about them is much more readily available than it was in the Sixties, and college and other not-for-profit development offices have become much more sophisticated about fund raising.

Nonetheless, people are still poring through foundation directories and calling up Guidestar on their computers as they mine for information about foundation prospects and then send them cold proposals. In fact, an entire cottage industry of proposal writers has sprung up—women and men who hire themselves out for substantial fees to not-for-profit organizations to compose these documents. Guess what? Many of them are still generating the same kind of impersonally negative responses.

Now, in fairness to the foundations that send these kinds of turn-down letters, let me quickly observe again that only a very small percentage of them have large staffs. According to the Foundation Center, in 2006 a full 83% had no staff, and most of the rest had only 1-2 paid employees. It's also important to remember, as I soon learned, that the vast majority restrict their grant making to the communities in which they are based. All of them are correct when they tell you that they receive far more proposals than they could ever begin to consider funding. Even back in the 1960s I recall a program officer at the Rockefeller Foundation telling me that his institution funded only one per cent of the requests it received, so I'm sure that the odds may be worse now. But that's not the issue.

To be sure, not-for-profits have to ask for money, and foundations exist to give it away, so one might hope that the whole business could be transacted cleanly and swiftly by mail—but it simply doesn't work that way. Raising money from foundations, like all worthwhile human pursuits, is all about relationships. Let me simply offer a single dictum to summarize what I've learned about the search for foundation funding: never send an unsolicited proposal to any foundation.

Some of you who are reading this chapter will quickly object and cite an example when a cold proposal actually did net you a foundation grant. I've actually got a few examples of my own. But I'm also willing to bet that the grant you received a) wasn't especially large; or b) probably came from a family foundation that employs that mechanism for giving the same way you and I use a checkbook. In fact, if you can furnish me with a documented story to prove that you received more than $100,000 in response to a single, unsolicited letter, I'll refund the purchase price of this book.

If you're going to go chasing after foundation dollars, improve your odds by developing relationships with the people who run them before you begin submitting requests. That process often will involve taking circuitous routes: you may speak with a board member who knows someone else who is a close friend of a foundation program officer, and you will have to follow that thread of acquaintanceships as you seek an appointment to make your case. Even then, sometimes you'll have to send the foundation a brief, written synopsis about what you have in mind before you secure a face-to-face meeting. And yes, sometimes the reply to your inquiry will make it clear that you're not going to get an interview. However, big game hunters know the value of patient stalking and recognize that they're not always going to get a shot at their prey.

However, if you have a program or project that a foundation

considers worthy of support, the day will come when you gain admission to its offices. When that happens, engage its representatives in the fleshing out of your concepts. Spend as much time listening to what their interests may be as telling them about what you plan to do. These foundation officers will let you know when they want to see in a full proposal, and when they do, your submission often will be simply the written confirmation of an already negotiated agreement. A colleague who until recently directed the affairs of one of the South's largest foundations put it even more simply in remarks to a workshop a few years ago: a proposal is something for the files.

An Exception to the Rule

A few pages ago I shared some thoughts about the importance of establishing relationships with representatives of the foundations from which you are seeking support. In the drama below, the representative of a not-for-profit arts organization has successfully penetrated the inner sanctum of a large foundation by securing an appointment with one of its program officers. However, the "unspoken conversation" (in italics) that occurs is intended to serve as a reminder that grant seeking is an art and not a system of scientific principles:

(THE SCENE OPENS IN THE OUTER OFFICE OF A LARGE FOUNDATION. A RECEPTIONIST IS SEATED BEHIND A DESK AND LOOKS UP AS A GRANT SEEKER—THE DEVELOPMENT OFFICER FOR A SMALL, STRUGGLING, LOCAL ARTS ORGANIZATION—ENTERS THE ROOM.)

Receptionist:	Good morning. Mr. Smith will be with you in a few minutes. May I offer you some coffee?
Grant Seeker:	Yes, please. Black with sugar. [*God knows, I might as well take everything I can get while I'm here.*]

(RECEPTIONIST DISAPPEARS FOR A FEW MINUTES.)

Grant Seeker:	[*Will you look at this place? I could pay two staff salaries for the next couple of years for what it cost to decorate the reception area.*]

(RECEPTIONIST RETURNS WITH COFFEE IN PORCELAIN CUP WITH SAUCER.)

Receptionist:	Did you have any difficulty finding our offices?
Grant Seeker:	Not at all. [*Are you kidding? Every not-for-profit employee in the city memorized this address years ago. It's like asking a Muslim if he knows where Mecca is.*]
Program Officer:	(ENTERS ROOM) So sorry to keep you waiting.

I see you already have some coffee. Why don't you just bring it with you. (LEADS WAY DOWN HALL TO SUMPTUOUSLY FURNISHED OFFICE)

Grant Seeker: I appreciate you taking the time to meet with me.

Program Officer: Not at all. [*Damn, I hope this doesn't take too long. I've got work to do.*]

Grant Seeker: You have a beautiful office. [*That desk must be solid mahogany I wonder how much it cost.*]

Program Officer: Have a seat. It sure is a lovely day out there, isn't it? [*Why do we have to go through this small talk?*]

Grant Seeker: It sure is. [*Why do we have to go through this small talk?*] I really appreciate your taking the time to meet with me. [*Damn, I already said that.*]

Program Officer: Not at all. That's part of my job. [*Not my favorite part, to be sure.*] How long have you been with the theater?

Grant Seeker: It's been almost five years now. I came soon after we received the last grant from your foundation.

Program Officer: (REFERS TO FILE ON HIS DESK) Yes, at that time we gave you $10,000 toward the cost of your renovations. [*If the wife of our president's best friend hadn't been on your board at the time, you wouldn't have gotten a dime.*]

Grant Seeker: You sure did. [*Even though we asked you for $75,000.*]

Program Officer: So what would you like to discuss today?

Grant Seeker: We're very excited about a festival we've organized during which we'll be presenting a series of both one-act and full-length productions by playwrights throughout the state. It should be a wonderful way to showcase new talent and raise the city's visibility as a center of the arts.

Program Officer: [*Just what we need—a week's worth of unintelligible experimental plays by a bunch of anti-Establishment writers and producers!*] You're aware, of course, that most of our support for the arts takes the form of grants to the Elite Theatrical Center .

Grant Seeker: Yes, I am, of course. [*Where nobody will ever be offended by non-controversial productions and road show revivals off CATS.*] However, our market surveys suggest that there's a growing audience for alternative theater in the metropolitan area.

Program Officer: That's very interesting. [*In your dreams, fella. I don't know anyone who likes that crap.*]

Grant Seeker: (PULLS FOLDER FROM BRIEFCASE) Here's a copy of the marketing study that I'd like to leave behind for you to look over as well as a prospectus about the festival.

Program Officer: Thank you very much.

Grant Seeker: We would, of course, like to submit a formal proposal as soon as possible.

Program Officer: [*I'll bet you would.*] What's the projected cost of this...uh, festival?

Grant Seeker: It'll cost about $15,000 [*because we know how few funders in this town have any understanding about the importance of our work, so we're having to do it on the cheap.*]

Program Officer: Tell me a bit more about who else is planning to support it.

Grant Seeker: Well, all of our board members have made pledges. Their names are listed right there on the prospectus.

Program Officer: (STUDIES THE LIST) That's certainly very important. [*Who are these people? I've never heard of any of them.*] I see they've committed themselves to give a total of $3,000.

Grant Seeker: And of course we're developing proposals to many of the other foundations and businesses in the community. [*Or at least we will as soon as I can get out of here.*]

Program Officer: Yes, it's important to have as broad a base as possible. [*Good luck, pal.*] Well, I do appreciate you taking the time to keep us informed about your plans.

Grant Seeker: Would it be appropriate for us to submit a proposal, then?

Program Officer: As you know, we consider all requests.

Grant Seeker: We were thinking about asking for $7,500.

Program Officer: That, of course, is your decision.

Grant Seeker: [*What a cold fish!*] We'll get it to you by next week.

Program Officer: And we'll look forward to receiving it.

Grant Seeker: Well, thanks again for meeting with me. [*What a friggin' waste of time this has been!*]

Program Officer: Not at all. That's what I'm here for. [*I guess it could have been a lot worse; at least he didn't take too long.*]

Grant Seeker: Whatever happens, we also hope you'll plan to come to the festival. [*I won't hold my breath.*]

Program Officer: [*Yeah, right!*] Thank you very much.

Grant Seeker:	Have a good day. [*Let me outa here. I don't get paid enough to do this job.*]
Program Officer:	You too. [*I don't get paid enough to do this job.*]

All of the grant seekers with whom I shared this piece—including a former university president whose institution has garnered millions of philanthropic dollars from foundations—winced as they recognized themselves in the drama. What can I say? If you're going to approach foundations for support, there will be some periods of great awkwardness in which both parties recognize or at least suspect that they are not likely to have a shared future. And in fairness to program officers everywhere, I have many more stories of foundation representatives who have knocked themselves out to be supportive of new and interesting projects.

What are the lessons to be learned from this story? Obviously, one could hope that the program officer had been a bit more welcoming. Then again, the grant seeker might have been a bit more prepared and energetically persuasive. He might also have had more success if he had brought the wife of the president's best friend. As it turned out, one wonders whether both of them sensed from the outset that they were simply going through a set of obligatory, ritualized motions. Perhaps the final takeaway is that grant seekers cannot lose heart. Not every blind date leads to marriage—or even a romantic interlude. Not every business call produces a sale. You leave not-so-close encounters of this kind and comfort yourself with the knowledge that other prospects exist and that you will win over at least some of them.

Desperate Times; Desperate Measures

For all the "how-to" books and articles and other presentations on the subject of fund raising, success sometimes depends upon forgetting all the formulas and trying something different. To illustrate the point, here's one war story that I can't resist sharing.

###

Our $18 million national building campaign had started well. The largest private foundation in the city had made a lead gift of $7 million. The CEO of the international company that was the source of the foundation's wealth had agreed to be the national chairman of the campaign, and the president of one of the banks, who also sat on our board, volunteered to head the local fund raising effort. We assembled the requisite committees to support their leadership. Our campaign materials were rhetorically persuasive and graphically attractive. We had a strong case. It all looked like a slam dunk

In my role as the institution's chief development officer, I paid a call upon the national chairman in his sumptuous office at corporate headquarters. He assured me that he would sign any solicitation letter we might put in front of him, assigned his chief aide to be the liaison to our campaign, and graciously dismissed me. I never saw him again. He didn't even show up for the campaign kickoff. It was a warning sign of foul weather ahead.

True to his word, the national chairman did sign a lot of letters to corporate peers and the company's suppliers, and they did net us a few hundred thousand dollars in pledges and contributions, but I never was able to get him to follow up personally with any of the rest of the prospects.

On the strength of approaches to other local foundations and corporations—aided by the local chairman's vice president for community affairs (I didn't see much of the local chairman thereafter either)—we raised some more money. And on our own, my boss and I were able to pry loose some additional grants.

However, the hard, cold reality—after a year of work—was that we had raised barely $1 million. None of the other campaign committee members seemed inclined to do anything except come to expensive lunches and listen impassively to our pleas for help.

During that year the national chairman's liaison had been assigned to other duties, and I was now in the hands of another corporate vice president. He was a most pleasant gentleman with whom I later became friends. He and I would meet every few weeks so I could report on our "progress." He would listen attentively, but could offer little in the way of assistance; seemingly he had almost as little access to his boss as I did. These enjoyable but essentially meaningless encounters continued for several months, and my frustration and anxiety increased proportionately. We were going nowhere fast.

I can't remember exactly what triggered it, but during one of our meetings, as we sipped coffee and exchanged sweet fund-raising nothings (I had absolutely no progress to report that day), I heard myself say ruefully, "You know, if we don't meet our campaign goal, it's really going to reflect poorly on your boss and the company." He didn't reply, but I saw a shadow of concern cross his face. I filed away his reaction for future reference.

The next time we met I repeated my pessimistic warning. Then, for the next few times we got together, I would slump down in my chair, frown mightily, and morosely drone on about the potentially negative impact on the corporate image if the campaign were to fail. My colleague clearly was getting the point (he too was frowning more), but he gave no signal that my message was being transmitted anywhere else.

Summer came, and our respective vacations meant that we didn't see each other for a while. Then, out of the blue that fall, my office telephone rang late one afternoon. On the other end of the line was the president of the foundation that had made the lead gift to the campaign. Although his usual courtly and gracious self, he wasted little time in getting to the point. "How much money will it take to complete the campaign? he demanded. "About ten million dollars," I replied. "I'll get back to you," he said.

Suffice it to say that within less than a month, the so-called campaign was over. We had "raised" the requisite $18 million—nearly $10 million of it in the form of a personal gift from the foundation's creator to go with the $7 million from his foundation—and construction was underway. Today the facility we set out to build still stands as a tribute to one donor's extraordinary generosity, to a concern about corporate image, and—at least partially, I am bold enough to assert— to one development officer's desperation. At least that's the way I remember it.

Let's Have a Special Event

As we all know, one of the most important breakthroughs in the evolution of humankind occurred when our ancestors learned how to build fires. What a boon to everyone! All of a sudden there was a new way to stay warm, and folks didn't have to eat raw hamburgers any more. But like all good things, the art of fire-starting brought with it a new set of issues. Everybody from amateurs to arsonists was getting into the act. Fires were breaking out or being started all over the place, thereby wreaking havoc in the community.

It's my speculation, therefore, that the first not-for-profit organization in the history of the world probably was a volunteer fire department. I further suspect that the members of this hardy band of firefighters were very excited about their new mission when they got started. And the women's auxiliary members were equally proud of their contributions— which consisted primarily of stitching together animal hides to make the buckets that early fire brigades needed to pour water on the flames that threatened people's homes.

By this time, I would further speculate that some rudimentary form of cash coinage had also come into being, and the volunteer fire brigade began asking for contributions. Who knows? They may even have figured out a way to stop passing traffic and request donations to be dropped into whatever passed for boots.

However, as the years (decades? centuries? millennia?) passed and even more people learned how to start fires, the situation began to get out of control. The volunteer fire department had a growing list of needs: ladders, wagons, animals to pull the wagons. It all added up to more than could be supported by simple neighborly voluntarism and coerced contributions. Besides, the volunteers had grown weary of soliciting small change. One night the leaders of the unit assembled at their station to discuss the situation, and I'm willing to bet that somebody said, "Let's have a special event."

###

During the lifespan of almost every struggling not-for-profit organization, it is virtually axiomatic that someone will propose a special event. The rationale advanced by its proponent is that it will most assuredly rescue the organization from the miasmal depths of financial despair through which it is sloughing.

Many of you will recognize the situation. The organization, already in debt, is once again talking about fund raising—an activity no one relishes. Someone ventures the notion that what they need to do is put on a silent auction/concert/golf tournament. The advocate swears that his brother has a sister-in-law who knew someone with another not-for-profit who did something like this with great success.

I have organized my share of these fund raising events, and I dislike them intensely for a number of reasons. First, it still annoys me that some people apparently won't contribute to an institution or cause unless they receive something in return. The second reason is that very few of these events are especially cost-effective. If everybody who sold tickets, solicited items to be auctioned, or recruited foursomes for a golf tournament would instead have simply written a personal check, the organization would often net more money, and the time of the volunteers (and the staff members who have to coordinate their work) could be put to more useful purposes.

I know there are organizations that have developed special events into annual traditions which in turn have demonstrated their ability to raise significant sums of money. However, generally speaking, these dinner-dances or concerts or sporting events can count upon an audience composed of an already well developed list of constituents and donors who have been conditioned to purchase tickets and attend. Furthermore, these organizations usually have other sources of revenue; they don't bet the farm on a single event. And that's all fine.

But woe to the not-for-profit that believes its special event will snatch it back from the jaws of fiscal insolvency. I still recall the organization in a neighboring county that decided to eliminate its deficits by presenting a country music concert. It convinced the lead artist to contribute his time and talent, but nobody realized that his expenses, the cost of his back-up musicians and their travel expenses, and the printing and widespread distribution of promotional materials would add up to about \$30,000. And nobody understood the need to get financial sponsors for every expense item in the budget, so that all ticket sales would generate a surplus. The leaders naively thought that ticket sales could cover the costs and still net a profit. After all they had done the math. If they sold 2,500 tickets at \$25 each, they'd make \$62,500. After paying all the bills, they'd still have about \$30,000.

However, when the time came to mail out the expensive invitations, they were hard pressed to come up with more than 500 addresses of past donors and other friends. Furthermore, no one had checked to see whether the performer was popular enough to make people who read the posters or heard the radio ads want to come to the local arena and listen to him. Before the story gets too painful, let me simply note that this well-intentioned and poorly informed organization lost its entire investment in the special event and soon thereafter declared bankruptcy.

I have no illusions that my little tirade will stop anyone from attempting to organize a special event, so here are a few suggestions that may help to forestall a disaster:

- Insist that the people who propose the idea of a special event serve as its organizers and initial financial sponsors.

- Demand a budget that anticipates every contingency. (If a meal is involved, what will be the cost of flowers or other decorations for the tables; if a performer is coming, what will be the cost of hiring security; what will you do when those in attendance ask to have their parking tickets validated; what will the hotel or hall charge you for AV equipment; who's going to pay for the caps, shirts and balls that the golfers in your tournament will expect, not to mention their beer and snacks? The list goes on and on.)

- Secure sponsors for all of these items before announcing the event.

- Put together a list of people who can reasonably be expected to attend. If the revenue that their participation will generate is not significantly greater than a well-sponsored event will cost (in other words, if your net surplus is only going to be modest), shift your attention to raising your goal by simply asking the same people for that amount of money. (Years ago, some clever soul invented the non-event, which involved inviting people to a banquet that was not going to happen and asking them to pay for the privilege of not attending. Those receiving the invitation were sufficiently grateful not to spend an evening this way that they responded generously. The idea was widely copied and eventually ran its course, but its inventor was on the right track.)

There actually are justifiable reasons for some special events that have to do with important matters like building good will, recognizing the contributions of major donors, achieving greater visibility, or celebrating an historical milestone in the organization's history. However, think long and hard before planning and organizing one of these galas or benefits as a principal source of revenue or a way to rescue your organization from a deficit.

Somewhere over the Rainbow

If you're employed by a not-for-profit organization or have been a volunteer board member of one (especially if it's relatively small), it's almost inevitable that the subject of building an endowment has arisen.

As often as not, it begins this way. The board has convened, and the Finance Committee chair has delivered the typically dismal report. Expenses exceed income, the budget has been trimmed to the bone, and no relief is in sight. A board member (typically one who makes only sporadic financial contributions and has never solicited anyone else), clears his throat and pontificates, "If we had an endowment, we wouldn't always be in this position of having to live from hand to mouth." This remarkable piece of profundity quickly captures the imagination of others around the table who excitedly climb on the bandwagon. "He's right. We need an endowment." "None of us is any good at asking for money anyway, and when we do, the people we go to are already over-committed...." "An endowment would ease a lot of the pressure." "Every strong not-for-profit has an endowment."

After several more minutes of this self-reinforcing babble, another board member looks at his watch, reaches for his jacket, and grandly proclaims, "I'd like to move that we begin an endowment campaign." The chair calls for a second, gets it, and the motion passes unanimously as all of those present nod gravely. The meeting adjourns. The board members beam with self-satisfaction about their collective wisdom. They say their good-byes and leave the room.

Permanent endowments are the pot of gold at the end of the rainbow for many not-for-profit organizations. All of us in the field gawked with incredulous envy when Harvard University's portfolio hit the $34 billion mark and lusted after a similar state of fiscal security. However, perhaps some cautionary words about the search for endowments by the average not-for-profit organization are in order. In no particular order, here they are:

- An endowment is no substitute for an ongoing program of fund raising from a wide base of support. The existence of Harvard's umpteen billion dollar endowment hasn't led it to disband its large and energetic development staff. Indeed, I suspect that many of its endowment gifts came from individuals who began as donors to the annual fund.

- The organizations most likely to attract endowment gifts are those—like universities—that give promise of being around for a long time. Usually they can offer that promise because they've already been around for a long time. The recently established Center for the Electronic Arts or the Hospice for German Shepherds are not notably strong candidates for contributions that will continue in perpetuity.

- People make endowment gifts to institutions for which they feel a particular sense of loyalty or gratitude. That's why alumni establish permanent legacies at their alma maters, why wealthy cancer and heart disease survivors endow new wings at the medical centers that cared for them, and why parishioners establish lasting funds to support their beloved churches and synagogues.

In short, if you don't have a large base of established donors who feel a strong sense of loyalty to your well-established organization, your odds of building a major endowment are generally slim.

Here are some other thoughts to consider.

- Relatively few professionally managed foundations make endowment grants. One executive with whom I once explored the notion of endowing something put it this way, "Why should we transfer $1 million from our portfolio into yours? We'd just as soon have you continue coming to us with your proposals. Besides, we can afford better investment counsel than you can."

- Virtually all endowments are created by wealthy individuals or families. Although it is understandable and even heart-warming when a group of individuals seeks to establish an endowment fund to memorialize a dear-departed friend or colleague, the results invariably sputter out after the first few thousand dollars have been raised.

- Donors of endowment funds rather like the notion not only of perpetuating the institutions to which they give but also purchasing a measure of personal immortality for their names or the names of close relatives—preferably on buildings in letters that are easily recognized from some distance away or on scholarships, professorships, lectureships, and major programs and events.

Please don't misunderstand. I love endowments, and I have helped to raise endowment funds… from loyal supporters on behalf of well-established institutions that already enjoy a secure financial position. Put most baldly, an endowment drive is not a substitute for a strong annual fund raising program.

In some cases, endowment gifts may carry with them the distinct threat of destroying the institutions they are meant to help. Here's a true story: A wealthy member of a small congregation in coastal Georgia died and left his church a legacy of some $60 million. The relatively young but clearly wise pastor recognized immediately the inherent danger of a gift that could lead his flock to stop its regular giving. He convinced the lay leaders to use the funds instead to establish a private foundation to which the church, like other not-for-profit organizations, could apply for special needs. (His good sense went event further: the new foundation's by-laws stipulated that the pastor could not be the foundation's executive and that the regional bishop of the denomination could not be a member of the board.)

In brief, then, if you're the board member of the "typical" not-for-profit organization, think carefully before devoting a lot of time to organizing an endowment campaign. If you're the executive of the organization, and board members insist upon promoting the notion of endowment building, invite them to demonstrate their commitment to the concept by establishing the first permanent legacies.

MANAGING THE CHARITABLE DOLLAR

I am an unapologetic advocate for the not-for-profit sector and its importance for the preservation of our democracy. I stand in awe of the caring, hard-working, usually under-paid staff and the dedicated volunteers who keep these mission-drive organizations functioning.

The smaller, usually locally-focused ones face all kinds of governance and management challenges. Few of them are able to recruit the kind of board members who customarily guide the affairs of, say, major symphony orchestras and museums. Because the salaries they can offer generally are low, the staff members they can attract are often young and inexperienced. Yet they soldier on.

Their motivations vary, of course, but some of it has to do with the company they get to keep. If what my friends in the for-profit sector tell me is true, many of their dealings are with people who—if not unethical—push the moral envelope pretty damn hard. Those of us often under-paid, not-for-profit types at least don't have to spend a lot of time dealing with scumbags.

From the perspective of the for-profit world, the professionals and volunteers in the not-for-profit sector may not always seem to be the most organized. However, that "failing" all too often is a function of the limited resources available to them. Folks who are driven by a "bottom-line" orientation sometimes castigate these not-for-profit practitioners for not being sufficiently "realistic." I would instead prefer to praise these men and women for having the compassion and the vision to imagine a far better world for everyone and the passion to keep working to bring that world into being. Because not many of these good people are motivated by the need for the big bucks, they are freed to focus their energy upon the task of community service.

I recently came across an article by an academic who postulated the serious shrinkage of the sector. For a variety of reasons, he argued that lots of not-for-profit organizations—those million-plus not-for-profit organizations that play a principal role in holding together our democracy—are not going to be able to sustain themselves and therefore will go out of business. I think he's way off base. To be sure, not-for-profit organizations will come and go; they always have. Darwin's thesis about the survival of those best able to adapt applies to this sector too. However, the American propensity to form associations for all kinds of charitable purposes is too deeply ingrained in our national character to experience significant change. Not long ago, I heard Diana Aviv, the CEO of Independent Sector, report that 72,000 new not-for-profits come into existence annually.

Furthermore, there will continue to be an enormous need for not-for-profit organizations that respond to the needs of their fellow citizens in ways that government cannot do or refuses to do. In some ways, for all of our often criticized political naivete, our documented disinterest in voting, and our rugged individualism, many Americans are remarkably fine citizens—at least as measured by their willingness to respond charitably to the needs of their neighbors. No, the not-for-profit sector will remain alive, energetic, and necessary for our country.

The Perfect Not-for-Profit Chief Executive

Not-for-profit chief executive officers direct the affairs of museums, homeless ministries, schools, membership organizations, advocacy groups, ballet companies, literacy programs, migrant worker services, homes for the elderly...the list goes on and on. Most of them do so because they care deeply about the people they serve and/ or the causes that their organizations promote. At the same time, as chief executive officers they have the same kinds of core management responsibilities as the leaders of for-profit corporations.

Serving as the CEO of a not-for-profit organization is not a job for the faint-hearted. Even if you're employed by a major university or a national relief association, the pressures can be enormous. However, I reserve perhaps my deepest respect for the leaders of much smaller educational, human service, arts, and other not-for-profit agencies and organizations. For them the major monthly challenges include not only faithfully fulfilling their institutional missions but also keeping the lights on and meeting payroll.

It's fascinating to read the job descriptions that many not-for-profit organizations circulate when they launch searches for new CEOs. Generally speaking, as a friend of mine put it, they seem to be looking for Jesus Christ with an M.B.A. Not-for-profit executives are expected to bring with them a wide range of human relations, managerial, financial, fund raising, planning, communications, and entrepreneurial skills—and be willing to do so for compensation that is often far below what those same skills would attract in the for-profit marketplace. The good news about the sector is that I have met a rather large number of wonderful individuals who actually do perform most of these functions at exceptionally high levels.

BoardSource and other organizations have produced a wealth of publications that lay out the necessary skill sets for first-rate executives. I have no intention of replicating their work. However, I have given some further thought to what I consider the most valuable attributes of successful CEOs. The result is a rather short list:

- They love their work and believe passionately in their organizations' missions.

- They can articulate a vision of what their organization could be and do and also are able to convince others to share that vision and implement the steps toward achieving it.

- They hire colleagues or recruit volunteers whose skills will enhance their own and then give them a great deal of independence to do their jobs.

The fact that they direct the work of "do-good" organizations naturally does not absolve them or their boards from the duty of maintaining well-run operations (and I have more to say about that subject a bit later in the book). One of the ways in which growing numbers of them exercise this responsibility is to submit to regular reviews of their work. At the Southeastern Council of Foundations, I annually prepared a self-evaluation of my performance during the past year for my board members and in turn submitted to a parallel review of my achievements by them. It's a highly important exercise, and I commend it to all organizations.

Nonetheless, I have also sometimes wondered whether this review honestly captured everything that was going on behind the scenes. Back in 2001, the Forum of Regional Associations of Grantmakers was preparing for its annual summer gathering of chief executive officers, scheduled to be held in Kennebunkport, Maine. The planning committee asked me to prepare a session on "The Perfect CEO."

I did a bit of research in the literature about leadership and came up with statements like "the leaders most in demand are those who understand the essential difference between the old way of 'managing by ordering' and the new way of 'winning by supporting and empowering.'"—all of which struck me as interesting but a bit stuffy. Instead of trying to be abstract and academic, I decided to have a little fun by composing a new kind of performance measurement. I have since amended the thoroughly unscientific survey that follows to make it a bit more generic. If you're a CEO, you might enjoy taking a few minutes to complete it and see whether you learn anything about yourself.

"HOW'M I DOIN'?" SURVEY

	SCORE
1. I have been the chief executive officer of my organization for: More than 7 years. 10 points At least 3 but less than 7 years. 8 points At least 1 but less than 3 years. 4 points I don't remember how long I've been here, but I wish to God that I could afford to quit. (Subtract) 10 points	_____
2. I was hired: On the basis of a national search. 10 points On the basis of a local search. 8 points Because my predecessor anointed me. 4 points Because I'm related to a board member. (Subtract) 10 points	_____
3. I have given leadership to the creation of a board-developed long-range plan for our organization. 10 points We've finished the mission, vision and values statements; now on to the goals. 8 points One of these days I'm going to get to work on a long-range plan. 4 points Give me a break; I've been too busy putting out fires even to think about a strategic plan. (Subtract) 10 points	_____
4. During my tenure the number of clients served/programs conducted/audience size/enrollment/membership (pick the main objective category you use to measure success): Increased by more than 20% 10 points Increased by more than 10 but less than 20%. 8 points Increased by more than 5 but less than 10%. 4 points Decreased. (Subtract) 10 points	_____

	SCORE
5. My relationships with my board... ...are highly collegial 10 points ...are civil 8 points ...resemble protracted guerrilla warfare 4 points We're about 3-5 funerals away from having a board I can work with. (Subtract) 10 points	_____
6. One of the most important and enjoyable parts of my job is maintaining close relations with board members, keeping them engaged in setting policy, and informing them regularly about the work of our organization. 10 points It's not always fun, but I accept the fact that I need to maintain good working relationships with my board. 8 points I don't have much choice about working closely with the board; the members micro-manage everything. 4 points The less my board knows about what I'm doing, the more effective I can be. (Subtract) 10 points	_____
7. I look forward to board meetings. 10 points I am not upset by the prospect of a board meeting. 8 points The anticipation of a board meeting makes me highly nervous. 4 points Just the thought of an impending board meeting induces projectile vomiting. (Subtract) 10 points	_____
8. My entire board conducts a formal, annual review of my performance. 10 points The board chair conducts that formal review. 8 points Once a year, the board chair and I go out for lunch and informally discuss my performance. 4 points No one evaluates my performance, and that suits me fine! (Subtract) 10 points	_____

	SCORE
9. I know all of my staff members well and am thoroughly familiar with their job descriptions. 10 points I have a reasonably complete idea of what all my staff does. 8 points It's in my work plan to develop written job descriptions for everyone on my staff. 4 points Who was that person I saw in the work room this morning, and what does she do? (Subtract) 10 points	_____
10. Our staff is a tightly knit team that both works and plays together (e.g., celebrates birthdays; goes to ball games). 10 points My relations with other staff members are strictly professional but highly collegial. 8 points I tolerate most of my staff members because I can't afford to replace them. 4 points I'm trying to figure out how to fire at least two staff members or to make life so uncomfortable for them that they'll quit. (Subtract) 10 points	_____
11. I type my own letters, make coffee, know how to operate the copier and assist with mass mailings. 10 points If there's an emergency, I'm willing to pitch in. 8 points It's more cost-efficient to hire support staff to handle routine tasks and to use my time doing what I was hired to do. 4 points It is beneath my position to have to perform time-consuming and mundane tasks. (Subtract) 10 points	_____
12. I believe in hiring competent associates and delegating work to them 10 points I still feel the need to double-check and often correct the work of my staff. 8 points I approve all work before it is made public. 4 points Can't anybody in this office do anything right? (Subtract) 10 points	_____

	SCORE
13. I would willingly forego a pay increase if it would make possible increased benefits for my staff. 10 points I regularly seek to budget pay raises and increased benefits for my staff. 8 points I'm willing to consider staff requests for raises and improved benefits. 4 points Screw 'em. They'll get theirs after I get mine. (Subtract) 10 points	_____
14. I believe that holding regular and productive staff meetings is an essential part of competent management. 10 points Holding regular staff meetings is a necessary evil that is part of good management. 8 points I convene occasional staff meetings. 4 points Oh crap, it's time for another staff meeting. (Subtract) 10 points	_____
15. I regularly solicit suggestions from my staff. 10 points I welcome suggestions from my staff. 8 points I'm occasionally willing to consider staff suggestions. 4 points Staff suggestions are a negative reflection on my leadership. (Subtract) 10 points	_____
16. I have a thorough understanding of our finances. 10 points Our bookkeeper keeps up with the details of our finances and regularly provides me with an overview. 8 points I have a reasonably informed sense of what's going on. 4 points Balance sheets and cash-flow analyses are essentially a mystery to me. (Subtract) 10 points	_____

	SCORE
17. I believe and regularly remind my staff that our primary responsibility is to provide service to our "customers" in a cheerful and responsive fashion, and we do that. 10 points I and my staff respond to our customers' requests for assistance, although I sometimes wish they understood that we can't do everything they want. 8 points We do our best, but I've given up on trying to please everyone all of the time. 4 points This job essentially involves providing assistance to a bunch of willful, whining and ungrateful people (Subtract) 10 points	_____
18. I have instituted a comprehensive communications plan. 10 points We don't have a formal communications plan, but we do an adequate job of keeping everyone informed about our mission, goals and activities. 8 points We stay in touch with our customers and funders, but we don't have the resources to do much more than that. 4 points We're too busy to keep everybody informed; if you've got questions, we're in the phone book or check out our website. (Subtract) 10 points	_____
19. I willingly embrace the fact that a key part of my job is to balance the twin challenges of providing service and giving leadership. 10 points Trying to balance service and leadership is difficult but still important. 8 points Hey, some days I try to provide service, and other days I try to give leadership. 4 points It's impossible to provide both service and leadership without getting migraine headaches. (Subtract) 10 points	_____

	SCORE
20. The best part of my job is being able to work collegially with my board and staff to promote the causes to which we are committed. 10 points The best part of my job is being able to exercise my creativity through the development of new programs. 8 points The best part of my job is that I get paid regularly. 4 points The best part of my job is that I'm nearing retirement. (Subtract) 10 points	_____
21. I thoroughly enjoy being a not-for-profit CEO. 10 points I'm working hard to get this organization running so well that I can enjoy being its CEO. 8 points I'm willing to do what I'm doing until I get a better offer. 4 points Take my job, please!! (Subtract) 10 points	_____
TOTAL SCORE	_____

SCORE INTERPRETATIONS

168-210 points	You were born to be a not-for-profit CEO, and you should console yourself with the knowledge that you deserve a big raise (even though you're not going to get one).
130-167 points	You're doing a good job, but there's room for improvement.
84-129 points	You're hanging in there, but you may want to give some thought to attending a few management workshops.

Fewer than 84 points? Are you sure this job is for you??

It's Time for the Board Meeting

Over the past 35 years I have served on a fair number of not-for-profit boards. I've also chaired the governance bodies of a local adult literacy program, a performing arts company, a senior services center, the Forum of Regional Associations of Grantmakers, and the national advisory committee for a post-Katrina relief fund. Most of the women and men with whom I shared these oversight responsibilities were high-minded, thoughtful and even visionary leaders. A very small number were idiots. The rest were loyal, faithful troopers who did what they could to help struggling outfits whose zeal to do good far exceeded their resources.

I greatly admire these individuals who carve out time from their already busy schedules to meet regularly, review budgets, develop strategic plans, offer helpful suggestions, make financial contributions, assist with fund raising, and serve as ambassadors for the organizations they govern. Those with special legal, accounting, communications, and other skills frequently give beyond the regular call of duty and perform tasks that normally would fall to staff members—if the organization could afford additional employees. All of them take very seriously their ultimate responsibility to ensure that their organizations rigorously adhere to their legal obligations and faithfully stay true to their missions.

A veritable library of books describes in detail the responsibilities that fall to board members of not-for-profit organizations (e.g., hiring and evaluating the CEO, approving and monitoring budgets), so I won't bother to repeat them. Along the way, though, I have formulated my own set of gifts that I have seen in the best not-for-profit board members.

- They share a passion for the mission of the organization. They don't accept election to the board with an eye toward fattening their resumes or serving other personal agendas.
- They read—and absorb—the materials they receive from the organization, thereby preparing themselves to be able

ambassadors for it. When they don't receive sufficient material, they are quick to request that they need to be better informed.

- They support the executive and the staff, but they stop short of trying to micro-manage the details of day-to-day organization matters.

- They not only evaluate the CEO on a regular basis but also conduct periodic self-analyses of themselves as individual board members and as a governing body.

Serving on the board of and contributing to the sustenance of a well-functioning not-for-profit can be a very happy experience, as well as a way to become better acquainted with a new circle of productive and energetic leaders—some of whom may become great friends. The experience has been very instructive, and I have learned a great deal from many of my colleagues.

Nonetheless, I have also been intrigued by the way in which many otherwise very intelligent men and women, often from the business world and the professions, seemingly manage to suspend all the wisdom that has made them successful in their own work when they join not-for-profit boards. My cynicism about boards behaving at their worst generally doesn't last, but I did feel moved one day to jot down the following outline of a board meeting to illustrate disfunctionality at the not-for-profit governance level. See if any of it sounds familiar.

The board convenes, comes to order and approves (usually with nit-picking corrections) the minutes of the last meeting.

The CEO delivers her report and is quickly subjected to a lot of questions (many of them bordering on micro-management).

The treasurer reviews the organization's financial situation, still awash in red ink.

Several board members offer a series of suggestions about picayune ways to reduce expenses (e.g.,. re-use paper printed on only one side; hand-deliver all mail addressed to people within five blocks of the office; further reduce the hours of the already overworked, part-time secretary/bookkeeper).

The communications, program and benefit golf tournament committees offer their reports and recommendations—most of which are roundly discussed and significantly altered by the rest of the board.

All of this activity has consumed most of the time allotted to the meeting, and several of the board members are beginning to gather their papers in preparation for a swift departure while the rest are glancing at their watches. Only ten minutes remain until the agreed upon adjournment.

Still to be heard is the development committee report. As he has for the past three meetings, the chair distributes a list of wealthy prospects to be solicited. He asks his colleagues to review the list and let him know which of these potential contributors they are willing to approach for support. They stare at the names in awkward silence.

Finally, one brave soul clears his throat and says, "Face it, most of us don't have any close ties to any of these people or organizations. What if, instead, each of us would make a list of 10 of our personal friends and associates and approach them directly for a gift?"

His colleagues look at him as if he had asked them to perform an unnatural act. After more awkward silence, another board member volunteers a counter-notion. "Perhaps," she observes, "we need to recruit some new board members who do have the kind of connections that will get us closer to the wealth of this community."

This notion quickly gains some traction among her colleagues. Before adjourning the meeting, they direct the executive director to prepare a list of prospective new board members and bring it to the next meeting. (It should be noted that none of those present offers to resign.) Left behind in the now empty room is the executive director. She quietly pounds her head on the table and wonders whether she has enough bourbon at home to get her through the night.

Before concluding this essay, I'd like to take note of one kind of not-for-profit board that doesn't seem to have attracted a lot of attention and about which I feel the need to reflect for a few paragraphs.

The way it comes into existence often dooms it either to limited usefulness or a short lifespan. I am referring here to the not-for-profit that emerges because a typically visionary leader sees a need to be met and takes it upon himself/herself to organize an agency to respond to that need. The organization in question may be a school, a theater company, or a human services agency.

Generally speaking, these high-minded leaders recruit boards of directors by reaching out to close friends and colleagues who share or can be taught to share their passions for the causes they espouse. Therein lies the potential seed of destruction, because these often charismatic leaders don't really want oversight of their work; they seek enthusiastic endorsement of their ideas. Sooner or later, it is inevitable that some members of these recruited boards will take issue with some of the executives' ideas. Because these board members were essentially appointed by those same executives and not elected by their peers, they usually have no way to exercise their veto power. These organizations, whatever the by-laws may state, essentially belong to the founding executives. Whatever happens either has to be their way, or it's the "highway" for dissenters.

I have been asked to serve on several boards of this kind. Some of them have evolved into well-run organizations, although that seldom happened until the executive chose to leave. I have resigned from others when it became clear that I was expected to blindly accept the dictates of the CEO and not offer critical suggestions. If you're recruited to join the board of an institution that has been created by one of these cultic leaders, the greatest service you can perform to yourself, the founder, and the organization is to establish from the outset the ground rules under which you're willing to contribute.

With all of that in mind, I hope that many more talented men and women will join the ranks of those valuable individuals who govern the not-for-profit organizations of our country. It is a tradition of service that continues to be vital for our way of life.

You Need to Run This Place Like a Business

I'd like to propose some thoughts about the responsibility of all not-for-profit organizations to be highly accountable. However, before I begin lecturing, I need to get something else off my chest.

If you hang around the not-for-profit sector long enough, one of the platitudes you'll hear with some regularity goes something like this: "Not-for-profits need to be run like businesses." Like a lot of platitudes, it has the ring of common sense. After all, a successful not-for-profit, like a for-profit venture, needs to be well organized and to have a plan. Budgets, job descriptions, smoothly-run meetings, and client service all are necessary elements for a well-oiled operation.

For many years, I unquestioningly accepted the proposition that the not-for-profit world should emulate its for-profit counterpart. However, the more I thought about it, the less apt the analogy became. Of course, the major distinction between them is that the not-for-profits exist for completely different purposes. There also are some other obvious and perhaps superficial differences. Corporate leaders don't generally type their own letters, brew their own coffee, make their own travel reservations, and do their own filing. Not-for-profit leaders certainly don't get salary bonuses and stock options even when their enterprises operate with a deficit.

If the average not-for-profit organization had the funds available to most large corporations just for business entertainment, they'd all be operating in the black. Most not-for-profit leaders I know are absolute wizards at squeezing productivity from inadequate cash flow and underpaid and overworked staff. They are geniuses at securing in-kind contributions of equipment and furniture and shopping for bargains on office supplies. They routinely juggle the resources available from limited income and hold short-term creditors at bay. Many of them are just as entrepreneurial as their colleagues on the for-profit side of the fence.

Now that I've done some defensive venting, let me move on. I spent most of the past 11 years working with foundation folks.

However, from time to time I was asked to speak to groups of not-for-profit organizations that devote a great deal of their energy to looking for the grants and contributions that will keep their operations alive and functioning. When I did so, I often devoted a few minutes to the importance of good management and fiscal controls. I was especially comfortable at sermonizing about this subject, because I am one of the worst sinners when it comes to the failure to practice exemplary management.

It's true. Worrying about whether my personal or organizational accounts are balanced to the penny has never cost me a moment of sleep. Our organization had a budget of about a million and a half dollars, and I figure if we were within a few thousand dollars of where we were supposed to be, all was well. Fortunately for me, a couple of my volunteer treasurers shared that sentiment, although my feelings must have had the ring of outright heresy to the one C.P.A. who held that position during my tenure.

I do pride myself on usually having a well developed intuitive sense of where things stand financially, which is to say that I really didn't spend money that we didn't have or couldn't anticipate. To be sure, our organization was blessed with modest surpluses and enjoyed the fiscal buffer of a comfortable reserve fund. As a result, I could afford not to sweat all of the details.

During the final eight years on that job, though, I became increasingly scrupulous about studying balance sheets and cash flow statements and having answers to questions about our financial state of affairs. It all went back to a trustees' meeting in the third year of my employment when my report to the board made it abundantly clear that my disinterest in the details of our bookkeeping was perhaps a tad cavalier. The chair quietly noted that he and his colleagues might be more inclined to take more seriously my visionary rhetoric about the directions in which I wanted to move our organization if they had more confidence in my attention to the more mundane pieces of our organization's life. That reprimand stung, but he was, of course, correct.

I seemed to have forgotten my own experience with red ink—the days of working with clients who couldn't afford to pay my fees on a timely basis because of what sometimes is politely referred to as negative cash flow. It's a sad fact of life that far too many not-for-profit organizations live on a hand-to-mouth basis, always scrambling to pay the rent or to meet the payroll. On some occasions, I know the situation has made executive directors desperate enough to employ foolish or even illegal measures—like neglecting to send withholding taxes on salaries and wages to the government.

As a result, I exhort those in the grant-seeking portion of our sector to continue to be driven by their beautiful missions that are rooted in caring and compassion and the desire to bring about transformational change. However, I also caution them never to use those missions as an excuse for sloppy disregard of good management practices. If anything, given their narrow margins for error and the fact that they have been entrusted with support from others, they need to be even more painstakingly diligent than their for-profit counterparts.

FOUR CURMUDGEONLY ASIDES

The next four reflections appear in this book for one reason only—I want to get them off my chest and into print. I can further justify their inclusion by noting that a) I know many readers will be able to identify with what I've written, and 2) although the not-for-profit sector is a highly serious and important enterprise, we all occasionally need to step back from our labors and laugh at ourselves. If some of my opinions come across as curmudgeonly, let me simply observe that I've reached the age at which I consider occasional crankiness to be a virtue.

Worthy of Our Hire

During the past 20-some years, a virtual parade of women and men of all ages trooped through my office for what are currently called "informational interviews." All of them were impressively sincere about wanting to find a niche in the not-for-profit sector and to make a positive contribution to society. I especially enjoyed the enthusiasm and commitment of the younger visitors.

Periodically folks came by to discuss the possibility of second careers. They were tired of the corporate or professional grind; their jobs no longer offered them any meaning; they wanted to spend the rest of their working lives doing something they considered to be worthwhile.

At some point in these conversations, I gently raised the question about what sort of compensation they would like to receive if they were to take this altruistic detour. On many occasions, the figures they proposed (which, they quickly explained, would represent significant pay cuts) exceeded what I was currently earning. I then described to them the general salary ranges of our sector. I often was reminded of the story in the New Testament about the young ruler who came to Jesus for advice about finding eternal life. Jesus told him to sell all that he had and distribute the proceeds to the poor. As the story relates, the ruler became sad, because he was very rich. On some occasions, my visitors too became sorrowful and left.

I can relate. I'm not being judgmental about their inability to make the transition. Very few of us in the not-for-profit sector are completely pure at heart. Offhand, I can think of only three or four friends who forsook virtually all worldly possessions to work on behalf of the poor and disenfranchised. For better or worse, those of us who have labored many years on the not-for-profit side of the street feel that we deserve adequate compensation to support ourselves and our families. One of my favorite cartoons, spotted many years ago, depicts a thirty-something speaking to a friend and declaring, "What I'm looking for is basically the liberal dream. I want to do good and still get a piece of the action."

To be sure, there are some not-for-profit executives who, to my way of thinking, are paid way too much. A cynic might respond that my idea of what constitutes "too much" income is any amount that surpasses what I was earning when I left full-time employment. It's possible. I used to note that my financial goal in life was to retire at a salary equal to what a young associate makes during his first year at one of Atlanta's most prestigious law firms—a goal that I never achieved. In other words, my 40+ years of experience finally brought me to the lofty fiscal pinnacle of being worth less than some ambitious, smart-ass kid from Harvard who's working like a serf and dreaming of becoming a partner and living off his share of the earnings of a bunch of other smart-ass kids just out of law school.

Am I bitter? Not really. Do I think our values are all screwed up? Absolutely. It's all relative, of course. Toward the end of my career I was earning much more than public school teachers and law enforcement officers, and I didn't have to cope with a bunch of unruly kids or put my life on the line every day I went to work.

I have learned to accept the seeming judgment of many folks in the for-profit sector that we in the other sector are either unrealistic dreamers or fools. However, I do take umbrage at folks from the for-profit sector who seem to believe that we're in this line of work because we're incapable of holding down a real job. Oh well, that's a topic for another time and place.

Since my life in the not-for-profit sector has clearly not made me financially independent, I've been wondering what I'm going to do to augment those monthly Social Security checks now that I'm semi-retired. The options stretch across a broad spectrum. One end of it is the fantasy of being elected to the board of a foundation that provides its trustees with a generous annual compensation package (although a later chapter explains the problem with that option). The other involves going to live at the Open Door (an Atlanta-based, residential Christian community whose members minister to the homeless and people in prison). At the latter venue I would be assured of food, clothing, shelter, and a stipend of $50 per month. In return, I would be expected to help prepare meals for people who live on the street, perform housekeeping duties, and participate in occasional peaceful protests. All in all, it strikes me as a fair deal, although my wife still isn't convinced.

Thank You for This Opportunity to Speak to You Today

While directing the affairs of the Southeastern Council of Foundations, I was regularly deluged by a flood of letters, brochures, and e-mails from speakers' bureaus, usually based in Washington or New York, that offered our organization the opportunity to obtain the services of one of their clients. These women and men generally were well known authors, former elected officials, ex-generals or "motivational speakers." All of them commanded a fee of at least $25,000 plus expenses to show up and deliver a speech that they probably had already given to the annual conference of the Amalgamated Pipe Threaders Union or the national sales meeting of the Diddely-Doo Novelty Manufacturing Company in Las Vegas or Maui. I, of course, threw these tantalizing offers in the trashcan; as the CEO of a not-for-profit membership organization, I could think of much more useful ways to put that kind of money to work.

Nonetheless, when I discarded these promotions, I sometimes fantasized about what it would be like to be on that kind of speaking circuit. After all, the opportunity to deliver a few speeches annually and take home a six-figure stipend is not something to sneeze at.

If you labor in the not-for-profit vineyard long enough and develop a few sets of competencies, chances are that you too will be called upon periodically to deliver speeches. However, the vineyard generally expects its laborers to deliver their remarks for free or for little more than travel expenses. As a result, many of us have become quite adept at convincing our peers and colleagues to take additional time from their already overworked schedules and to prepare interesting programs and presentations for our meetings and conferences.

Some of us have more difficulty than others in saying "no" to these invitations. Sure, one of the reasons we agree to speak is ego-driven; it's always nice to have a captive audience. I'd like to believe, though, that those of us who agree do so really want to help other not-for-profit organizations and their constituents by imparting some measure of useful wisdom or transferable experience. Complicating matters for me is that I always feel compelled to spend some time trying to tailor my remarks to the particular audience. I've never felt comfortable with a canned delivery. I wish I could be like a very nice fellow I know who managed for many years to get away with getting up and delivering the same "motivational speech" to Lord knows how many different groups. It basically consisted of what he described as the four key elements for success: 1) Show up for work. 2) Show up on time; 3) Show up in uniform; 4) Show up ready to play. To be sure, he delivered these dictates with great energy and some additional commentary, but that's it.

I have indeed, from time to time, received modest monetary honoraria for my presentations. However, it is much more common for my oratorical pronouncements to be appreciatively acknowledged by some form of in-kind compensation. I have received books and a Whitman's Sampler; a couple of clocks, and a lot of coffee mugs; as well as a paperweight, a keychain, a ruler and, once, two ties.

Perhaps my all-time favorite tale, though, is about the morning I rose well before dawn and spent the next four hours crafting a virtually new speech. As I recall, it had something to do with rural economic development. I then drove three hours to a conference at the University of Alabama to deliver that speech to two different audiences. It was well received, and after the second presentation, before leaving for the three-hour drive back to my home, I was called to the front of the room by some of the conference organizers and presented with a jar of peanut brittle. To be sure, it was a very large jar of peanut brittle— most of which I consumed on the way back to Atlanta—but incidents like that do make you question your true worth.

Why am I even bothering to share that story? I'm really not whining, because as I have noted elsewhere, I have a far easier life than a public school teacher or a policeman. And God knows that I in turn have importuned my colleagues to perform similar feats and then presented them with less-than-costly gifts. Perhaps I simply want to go on record as celebrating all of us in this line of work who take seriously the importance of building a strong not-for-profit sector and not counting the cost involved—and to note that if you can't laugh about these experiences, you're probably going to have a nervous breakdown.

The Noise of Solemn Assemblies

On a regular basis during the past four decades, I have packed my suitcase and traveled to large annual conferences of peers and associates from the not-for-profit sector—frequently wondering why I'm even bothering to go. What is this herd instinct that compels us to congregate by the hundreds and sometimes even thousands?

I know in advance what's going to happen. All of us will leave our homes and offices for airports around the country and board planes to the conference destination. Since we'll be flying at hundreds of miles per hour, it will be easy to convince ourselves that what we're going to do when we get there must be important.

We will pour into large ballrooms to listen to speakers who have been recruited because they offer promise of being highly informative or inspirational. At one of these plenary events, the presiding officer will announce that once again that the assembly has achieved a record attendance. The conference registrants will wander into resource centers where they'll stuff the free tote bags that bear the name of some corporate sponsor with the annual reports and publications of their peers as well as the free trinkets offered at vendor booths. Then they'll trek up and down corridors in search of a concurrent session from which they hope to gain insight—and, even more important, additional handouts to stuff into those already bulging tote bags. Apparently some folks measure the success of a conference by the amount they have to pay in excess baggage charges on the way home.

In the not-for-profit sector, an underlying maxim of these events is the importance of cramming every available waking hour with something of value (by which is usually meant a speaker, workshop, or panel discussion, preferably in a windowless, overly air-conditioned room). When lawyers and other professionals hold their conferences, they have no problem in concluding all business in time for everyone to get an early-afternoon tee time or appointment at the spa. Not-for-profit folks, figuratively speaking, generally seem to pack their hair shirts before leaving for these conferences; they seem to feel driven by the need to be unrelentingly receptive to yet another learning experience.

One of the highlights of the assembly may well be a gala evening at an aquarium, museum, or other local cultural center. There the attendees will sample the cuisine of and listen to performances by groups celebrating the area's ethnic and other diversity. (I recall a period some years ago when political correctness dictated that seemingly every conference I attended felt compelled to present the local gay men's chorus—all of the members in tuxedos and properly exuberant if not always musically polished.)

The conference schedule often includes an evening when the mob is on its own for dinner. It will disburse itself in smaller groups to local eateries—an exercise that will provide the opportunity over breakfast the next morning to compare notes and score points for having discovered the most unusual, gastronomically unique, or architecturally curious place in which to dine.

Over the years I've registered for more of these jamborees than I can actually remember. They've included denominational conferences, educational conclaves, gatherings of representatives from not-for-profit organizations, and assemblies of foundation folk. I've played a role in helping to stage a fair number of them myself. Fairness compels me to note that a few of them have even been memorable; many have not.

Budget-tightening pressures of late have led to the use of these events for the scheduling of pre-conference and post-conference meetings. ("We might as well take advantage of the fact that everybody's going to be there anyway.") The result is that you no longer simply arrive on time, register, and attend. Instead, you show up two days early and stay over an extra day so you can also be part of smaller board and committee meetings. By the time you finally get back on the flight home, you're brain-dead and you've gained ten pounds from the combination of too much consumption of food and drink and too little physical activity. You've also lost a week's worth of productive office time. Then again, on the positive side, you will have collected a suitcase-full of key chains, food samples, paperweights, and other *tschotkes* to distribute to your children or grandchildren.

The year-long preparations involved in organizing these round-ups would be worthy of a separate essay. If you've been on the planning committee for one of these events, you know what I mean. The logistical nightmares associated with recruiting speakers and presenters, negotiating with hotels, taking care of special dietary needs, arranging transportation for site visits, and looking after all of the thousands of other details associated with one of these conferences rival the preparations for the invasion of Normandy.

Each year as the Southeastern Council of Foundations would begin planning for its next major conference, I used to voice the speculation— to which no one paid any attention—that we could probably accomplish the same results if we simply booked the facility, announced the dates, and invited people to show up. I contend that we don't always need banquets, major speakers, and three days' worth of concurrent sessions as an excuse for people simply to meet, experience fellowship, share experiences, and thereby learn from each other.

Full disclosure probably demands that I also tell you that I already have booked my flight to another conference next month.

Eschew Obfuscation!

Do you remember *Cool Hand Luke,* that wonderful movie starring Paul Newman as the nonconformist who is arrested and sentenced to work on a chain gang? His rebellious and unrepentant refusal to follow orders finally prompts the Captain in charge of the prisoners, played by Strother Martin, to deliver one of the most-quoted lines in film history: "What we've got here is failure to communicate."

Well, the not-for-profit sector also suffers from failure to communicate. I don't ride too many hobby horses to death, but one that I will not stop whipping and spurring is my loathing of the stultifying jargon that permeates the vocabulary of our field .

Perhaps one should blame my fanaticism on a string of truly wonderful English teachers at Moorestown (NJ) Friends School and later Haverford College. It was they who first introduced me to a love and respect for the language. I also have to acknowledge the prominent role of Cates Cannon and Ann Przylemski, the city and assistant city editors of the Youngstown (OH) *Vindicator* when I was a reporter for that newspaper. Unchecked by any formal restraint, my feature writing for the college rag had escalated into colorful and sometimes even entertaining bullshit—long on style and usually short on substance. When I went to work for them, Cates and Annie quickly set to work to clean up my act. They sent back the first story they handed me— about a simple real estate transaction—three times before I shaped it into an acceptable, five-sentence, two-paragraph piece. The experience was profoundly humbling, and it was repeated more than once. In the process, though, I think I learned that the best declarative writing is clean, spare, and cogent.

At any rate, I believe that far too much of the language we use to exchange ideas in the not-for-profit sector does more to confuse than to clarify. Like the social sciences (whose inferiority complex, I suspect, led them to translate common-sense sentiments into arcane hogwash), too much of the not-for-profit world has elected to take a noble calling and smother it in obscuring cant. Sometimes it's just plain incorrect. Here's my all-time favorite example of improper usage:

I don't know how it started, but several years ago many people began to describe the process of submitting a formal request for financial assistance as "writing a grant." I don't think I'll ever win this battle, but, friends, let me repeat for the umpteenth time: You don't write a grant. A grant is something that a foundation awards to you. You write a proposal in the hope of receiving a grant.

Tony Proscio at the Edna McConnell Clark Foundation has earned well-deserved praise and popularity for his three books that have attempted to cleanse the language used by grant seekers and grant makers. Permit me to add my own brief gloss on the subject.

Stop using words and phrases like:

At the end of the day   *Multi-faceted*
Benchmark   *Paradigm*
Best practice   *Place-based*
Bottom line   *Prioritize*
Conceptual framework   *Proactive*
Core competencies   *Result-driven*
Expeditious   *Strategic fit*
Fast track   *Synergistic*
Game plan   *Think outside the box*
Knowledge management   *Value proposition*
Matrix   *Win-win*
Mindset

Is there anyone who hasn't discovered the joys of a little game called "Bullshit Bingo"? If so, here's the way you play it. Before (or during) your next meeting, seminar, or conference call, draw a square on a piece of paper. Divide the square into five columns across and five down. That will give you 25 blocks. Write one of the words or phrases from the above list in each block. Then, as the meeting or conference call moves forward, check off the appropriate block whenever you hear someone use one of them. When you have checked off five blocks horizontally, vertically, or diagonally, shout, "BULLSHIT!" Playing the game will improve your attention span and also relieve a great deal of tension and boredom.)

Then there's our old friend, "leverage." I once received a letter whose author was exploring ways in which we might collaborate. He suggested that we might "leverage each other." I'm still trying to figure out whether that was a sexual proposition—perhaps even grounds for an harassment suit.

A client once showed me a document that declared his organization's intention to have an "impact on the human infrastructure front." Huh?

I saw a brochure in which a consulting group reported that: *Organizations seeking to capitalize on the demographic change must deal proactively with a diverse workforce by examining their own internal cultures, human resource systems and management practices with a critical eye in order to identify any practice inconsistent with maximum productivity of all employees.* (As Dave Barry, the syndicated humorist, used to write, "I'm not making this up.")

The text went on to note that the consultants advocated a: *Research-based, customized, multi-faceted long-range plan to help organizations to develop an effective multi-cultural work environment.* To describe that sort of language as "academic" would be an insult to the Academy. It is gobbledy-gook.

I once heard the public relations director for a national organization tell a group of workshop participants that the reason for narrowing down campaign publicity to a few key messages was "to provide comfortability for spokespersons in communicating." I'm sorry, but this explanation only serves to elevate my "uncomfortability."

Be sparing in your use of works like:

- *Unique* (The author of *Ecclesiastes* was right: there really isn't that much that's new under the sun. By the way, you cannot modify the word "unique.")

- *Excellence* (By whose standards?)

Finally, please write in the active voice: Passive language is lazy, wordy, and sounds boring.

Don't write:	Do write:
It is anticipated that...	We plan to...
This program will be undertaken...	We will begin this program...
Emphasis will be placed on...	We will emphasize...

Garrison Keillor, the host of *The Prairie Home Companion*, which airs on National Public Radio (and also depends for its survival upon charitable contributions) makes a strong case for the proposition that the next best thing to good sex is sweet corn. I'm inclined to agree, and I would further nominate clean writing for the third position on the list of things that give me the greatest pleasure.

REFLECTIONS ON GENEROSITY

I have never met anyone whose life and behavior was completely governed by the spirit of altruism. All of us are guided by a variety of self-interests. Nonetheless, as this book already has tried to describe, our communities and our nation are blessed because many individuals cheerfully succumb to their charitable impulses and extend generosity to their fellow human beings.

I applaud every time that happens. From my perspective, any concrete demonstration of love for humankind by a gift or a voluntary act of kindness is both noble and ennobling. I further believe that a sense of responsibility for one's neighbor to be not simply a tenet of my religious faith but also one of the highest expressions of citizenship.

I continually witness the transformational impact that philanthropy has not simply upon the recipients of generosity but upon donors themselves. Time and again, I have seen individuals and families and, yes, even companies find new meaning in their lives as they have used a portion of their blessings to help improve the lives of their neighbors.

Why are some people generous? Philosophers and scholars have pondered the question for centuries. Here are a few additional thoughts about the subject.

The Giving Spirit

Two kinds of people inhabit the world. When asked what they would do if they won a $50,000,000 lottery, the first group's fantasies turn immediately to mansions, sports cars, yachts, and trips around the world. Members of the second cohort dream of creating foundations and using them to support the not-for-profit causes dear to their heart.

I belong to the second group. That doesn't make me a better person. It simply means that I was lucky enough along the way to discover the great pleasure associated with generosity. Sad to say, some people have never found it.

You may have heard the story about the not-for-profit agency that had never received a contribution from one of its city's most successful businessmen. After careful research of his financial status, it dispatched a high-powered volunteer to call upon him in his lavish offices. The volunteer (himself a generous supporter of the organization) delivered a highly persuasive pitch for support, and then shifted into high gear. "Our research," he said, "shows that even though your annual income is over two million dollars, you don't give a dime to charity. Wouldn't you like to give something back to the community with a contribution to our organization?"

The businessman, who had listened carefully to the presentation, thought for a moment and then he said, "First, did your research also show you that my mother is dying after a long, painful illness and has huge medical bills that are far beyond her ability to pay?

"Embarrassed, the volunteer mumbled, "Uh... no, I didn't know that."

"Secondly," said the businessman, "my brother, a disabled veteran, is blind and confined to a wheelchair and is unable to support his wife and six children."

The volunteer began to stammer an apology, but was cut off again.

"Thirdly, did your research also show you that my sister's husband died in a dreadful car accident, leaving her penniless with a mortgage and three children, one of whom is disabled and another has learning disabilities requiring an array of private tutors?"

The humiliated volunteer, now stricken with guilt for having paid this visit, replied, "I'm sorry, I had no idea," at which point his prospect concluded, "So... if I don't give money to any of them, what makes you think I would ever give to your organization?"

That businessman is not all that mythical a figure. He may not represent a majority of the population, but I could tell you stories in great detail about other people like him. You probably could too. Sometime when you're sitting at a bar, ask the person on the next stool what organizations they contribute to regularly. On occasion I have been pleasantly surprised by the response, but more often I am shocked by responses like "I give $20 to United Way every year" or "I put a dollar in the collection plate every Sunday."

By the same token, I am frequently astounded by the generosity of other Americans. Even though I can and sometimes do deliver lengthy raps on greed and stinginess, I have the privilege of regularly meeting men and women who really care about their fellow citizens and demonstrate it with their gifts of time, treasure, and talent.

At the risk of sounding like some feel-good article in *Reader's Digest*, I would add that generous people are happy people. Mal Salter, a former CEO of the Hartford Foundation, retired to Florida. Thereafter, though, he still kept his hand in the promotion of philanthropy by telling people about the option of making planned gifts to the local community foundation and other charitable organizations. When Mal addressed a group of potential donors, he was always quick to point out that anyone who established a deferred gift would live forever. To prove his point, he would then whip out a list of people who had made these kind of gifts and who continued to live full and active lives—often defying the actuarial tables. I'm not a psychologist, but I suspect that a deeper truth lies beneath that humor. Generous people are happy people, and happy people tend to live longer. (After completing this essay, I also learned about a survey conducted by Elizabeth Dunn at the University of British Columbia which documents that "those who spent money on others report greater happiness" than that enjoyed by those who do not.)

Let me further note that it's not just about money. A senior center whose board I used to chair started a new program. For years, like many similar organizations, it had been a place where older people could gather for fellowship, engage in exercise programs, enrich their minds through study and reflection, and receive the stimulation of arts and crafts programs—all good stuff. But this center decided to take the active engagement with getting older to a new plane. The core message of the new program was that the formula for successful living into old age goes beyond simple self-development; it is most fully realized in service to others.

By providing service opportunities, the Center was recapturing and re-articulating an ancient truth that is present in all of the world's religions as well as all of the findings of modern psychology. The hallmarks of a successful and happy life are a heart that is thankful for the blessings of being alive and a generous and giving spirit. These elements are true at any age, but they are especially important as one grows older—a time when it becomes tempting (for reasons of decreased mobility and increased fragility) to withdraw, to isolate oneself, to shun company. It is precisely when that temptation to retreat from life is strongest that the message of the opportunity to serve needs to be heard the loudest.

###

In the wine-growing regions of the world, there is an ancient practice that is repeated each year after the grapes have been harvested and crushed. The owner of the vineyard fills a cup with the new wine and ceremonially pours it back into the ground. It is a wonderful symbol of the fact that we cannot simply take; we must give something back to replenish the resources upon which we draw and depend.

Several generous businesspeople I have known claimed to have no particular religious reasons for their charitable behavior. When asked why they contributed to worthy causes and institution, they replied, "I felt I owed it to the folks who helped me to be successful. I'm only saying 'thank you.'"

Lawrence Gellerstedt, Jr. was the CEO of a major and highly successful construction firm in Atlanta. Yet virtually every workday, Larry spent the first couple of hours attending board and committee meetings of the not-for-profit organizations he served as a volunteer, making fund raising calls, writing solicitation letters, or otherwise contributing to the well-being of the city. He referred to these activities as paying his civic rent.

Gene Struckhoff, the Johnny Appleseed of the community foundation movement in the 1970s and 1980s, understood this proposition very well. He believed firmly that no self-respecting citizens should have the temerity to die without having made provisions in their wills for permanent endowment gifts to their local community foundation. It was their responsibility to contribute to the well-being of future generations in the city where they had prospered.

It should be a collective national goal of the not-for-profit sector to encourage every American to leave a philanthropic and, if possible, endowed legacy for the generations-to-come—whether through establishment of a fund at a community foundation, a private foundation, or the endowment of a college or other not-for-profit organization. We need to revive and widely broaden the "Leave a Legacy" program that not-for-profit organizations launched several years ago in many communities and states.

I don't think anyone is born with a generous gene. That's why I believe that generosity is a value that can and should be taught; that it is possible to acquire a charitable streak. Once upon a time many more young people were introduced to the virtues of voluntarism and learned the meaning of charity and *tzedakah* (mercy and compassion) in their churches and synagogues. (At the very least they had the kinds of mothers who someone has described as travel agents for guilt trips.) A lot of that still goes on, of course, but I'd like to argue that all of us need to be about the business of promoting compassionate giving.

Much of the Atlanta Braves' success in winning 14 straight division titles was due to an exceptionally strong farm system of minor league teams. In places like Greenville, Macon and Richmond, under the guidance of skilled coaches, young recruits honed their natural talents and practiced the fundamentals of baseball until they become second nature. As a result, when veterans retired or moved on to other clubs, their young replacements were ready to make an almost seamless transition into the vacated positions. Other professions and trades too have long relied on internships and apprenticeships to bring young people into their fields.

If the spirit of philanthropy is to become an even more essential ingredient of our nation's character, we all should play an active role in looking for creative ways to teach the women and men who will succeed us about the joys and challenges of systematic charitable behavior. Like professional ballplayers, plumbers, artisans, physicians, and ministers, the philanthropists and philanthropoids of tomorrow can benefit from coaching and training. I'm pleased that this notion is gaining in popularity:

- Years ago, the Council on Michigan Foundations, with the support of challenge grants from the W. K. Kellogg Foundation, launched the creation of youth councils around that state that are involved in both fund raising and grant making. It also developed an entire K-12 curriculum on philanthropy.

- To honor my predecessor at the Southeastern Council of Foundations, we established an interactive program for new and/or young foundation board and staff members to teach them something about the history of philanthropy and its role in our region as well as to give them an opportunity to reflect upon their own leadership styles.

- In Atlanta, a generous couple has established an institute of philanthropy and service learning at The Westminster Schools.

- The Virginia Beach Foundation gives young adults in its community the opportunity to build pooled donor-advised funds. While these young citizens contribute over time to the building of a corpus large enough to support grant making, it gives them the simultaneous opportunity to recommend distributions from another fund established for their use by older and wealthier donors in the area.

- In Columbia, South Carolina, several foundations, working with Junior Achievement, are teaching kids how to become philanthropists even as they're learning how to be capitalists and run successful businesses.

- Ted Turner's family foundation awarded a series of grants through several community foundations in locations where he has land holdings that involved young people directly in identifying the projects to be supported.

- Many family foundations now are grooming the next generation of trustees to prepare for and accept their governance responsibilities. One went so far as to take elementary school-aged members of the family on site visits and encourage them to record their impressions in crayon.

Who knows how early the effort could begin? When my wife and I entered the elementary school across the street from our home to vote one November, I noticed a small bank in the hallway, sponsored by a local commercial enterprise. There the children can establish savings accounts and, I assume, even make applications for loans. Clearly, some savvy marketer has found a way to educate youngsters early on about the use of financial institutions. Why shouldn't this same elementary school also have a small foundation to which the children might make contributions and from which they might disburse grants?

Ellen Sabin clearly sensed that young children are ready to learn how to give when she wrote *The Giving Book: Open the Door to a Lifetime of Giving*. This simple volume has the ability to inspire and teach young readers as they embark upon a journey into the world of compassion and giving. The body of literature about generosity seems to be on the rise. Amy Kass has edited two fine collections of reflections about philanthropy—*The Perfect Gift* and *Giving Well, Doing Good*. Jim Doherty in Richmond has published a collection of profiles on Virginia philanthropists called *In Praise of Giving*. The Southeastern Council of Foundations helped to produce *Hidden in Plain View*—a video on the history of Georgia philanthropy.

Many universities now have large-scale curricula in not-for-profit management, and a growing number of them are establishing courses in philanthropy as well. I hope the trend continues. At the very least, I'd like to speculate that history courses would take note of the enormous contributions by people like Andrew Carnegie and Henry Ford and Robert Woodruff and James Duke as well as the role of Northern philanthropy in the establishment of schools and colleges for African-Americans in the wake of the Civil War; that economics professors would devote some time to the way the U.S. tax system enables and even encourages individual philanthropy; that law classes would discuss the responsibility attorneys have (or so I believe) to inquire about their clients' charitable intentions when drawing up their wills or designing their estate plans. I'd like to imagine English professors including some of the many pieces of literature that deal with the charitable impulse on their reading lists.

In a nutshell, all of us need to be about the business of making philanthropic behavior as much a part of our culture as going to baseball games and eating apple pie.

Agents of Charity

Folks who have to raise money spend a great deal of time doing what is called "prospect research." The internet has simplified the process, but not-for-profit staff members and volunteers still devote long hours to combing through directories and data bases to identify wealthy individuals who could be prospective donors and scheming how best to make contact with.

A couple of decades ago, though, the tide began to turn. I have a little fantasy that it happened this way:

A not-for-profit CEO (it could have been the head of a university or a community foundation or a hospital) was reading the newspaper one morning. As was her habit, she focused mainly on the business and society sections with an eye toward identifying possible donor prospects for her institution. Suddenly she had a flash of inspiration. She said to herself, "I'm spending a lot of time trying to identify possible donors, wangling introductions to them, and then taking them to lunch to encourage them to give to us. There's got to be a better way to get next to them....Who knows them best? Hmmm. That would be their professional advisors—their attorneys and accountants and financial consultants and estate planners. What I need to do is to educate these advisors about how we can help them serve their clients."

The result of that brain flash led to a radical shift in the pursuit of donor prospects. My mythical heroine and her colleagues in the sector shifted the focus of their attention to attorneys, accountants, estate planners, investment advisors, and insurance agents, and the results have been dramatic.

When I first met the delightful Mal Bank back in the late 1980s, he was the chief legal counsel to The Cleveland Foundation (the oldest community foundation in the country), and he was way ahead of the pack. Decades ago, he already was energetically contending that attorneys and other professional advisors have the moral responsibility to ask their clients whom they assist with estate planning about their charitable intentions.

Mal was fond of noting that when he met with clients who were seeking advice, he first had to convince them of two facts: 1) that they are going to die someday (and it's amazing how many people live in denial of that eventuality), and 2) that when they did, the federal government was going to take a whole lot of their money if they don't make other provisions for its disposition. After that, Mal said, it was easy to talk to them about their philanthropic options.

A lot of community foundations have found another way to open the subject of charitable intent. Instead of approaching prospective donors with requests that they establish donor-advised funds, they instead find a way to pose this kind of question: "What causes or institutions are you passionate about?" This tack led Sandy Richardson and her colleagues at the Victoria Foundation on Vancouver Island in Canada to develop a tagline that beautifully expresses that foundation's philosophy and has since been widely copied by other community foundations throughout North America and elsewhere in the world. The foundation declares that it is about the business of "connecting people who care with causes that matter."

It's a pleasure to report that Mal is no longer a lonely voice in the wilderness. Growing numbers of professional advisors are discovering that it doesn't constitute a conflict of interest for them to ask their clients about their charitable interests. Obviously, they can't or shouldn't shill for a particular institution, but simply putting the question on the table is a service that their clients seem to appreciate. These advisors can be the catalysts to precipitate the movement of an enormous amount of money into not-for-profit organizations' endowments and operating budgets.

Of course, these advisors need to be knowledgeable about the different options available to their clients and the tax advantages associated with them. I believe that one of the most important programs we ever launched at the Southeastern Council of Foundations began with getting the Georgia Bar Association to approve a Continuing Legal Education (CLE) course on philanthropic options for its members. Similar programs now exist in nine of the states in our region. One of the "texts" for that course is something called the *Southeastern Toolkit for Giving*—a document that we virtually copied, with permission, from our colleagues at the Minnesota Council on Foundations.

One of the reasons this strategy has become a proven formula for success is a financial phenomenon that's occurring as I write these words. It's been going on for the past several years and will continue for several more decades. Paul Schervish and John Havens at Boston College's Social Welfare Research Institute have been researching what they first described as the "intergenerational transfer of wealth." In 1999 they issued a report entitled "Millionaires and the Millennium: New Estimates of the Forthcoming Wealth Transfer and the Prospects for a Golden Age of Philanthropy." Their study's conservative estimate was that more than $40 trillion would be passed on through planned gifts and bequests and that a significant portion of that amount would be directed to charitable purposes. Any figure with twelve zeroes after it is almost mind-numbing to me; I once heard my friend Peter Hero describe the money involved as "umpteen godzillion dollars." At any rate, it's clear that we are talking about an unprecedented level of wealth changing hands.

In my office, we saw accelerating evidence of this phenomenon during the past several years. The last living member of a family foundation in a small Southern city dies, and its assets jump overnight from $4 million to $40 million. The sale of a family business turns a $3 million foundation into one with assets of $300 million. Community foundations have been acquiring hundreds of millions of dollars in donor-advised funds. It's all very exciting, especially for those of us in an historically poor region like the South.

However, I'm not naïve. Foundation giving, even if it increases exponentially, will still be a drop in the bucket when compared with individual giving, and will continue to be overshadowed by government support of the institutions and programs and projects we all care about. Nonetheless, the role of foundations in the building of strong and caring communities has the potential to be felt in ways never before imagined.

You can read the report for yourself, but what I find most interesting about it are some observations that come at the end of all the financial calculations. Read what these two scholars noted in conclusion:

> ...the economic and emotional incentives to devote financial resources to charitable purposes increasingly shape the moral sentiments of wealth holders; and [there is] a new values-based approach to financial planning that is increasing the commitment of wealth holders to charitable giving by guiding them through a planning methodology in which they discern for themselves: a) their material potential for charitable giving, b) the people and causes for which they care, and c) the combination of financial, family, and philanthropic strategies best suited to implement their objectives.... The recent shift in the proportions allocated, especially by the super wealthy, away from heirs and toward philanthropy have occurred in the absence of any changes in estate taxes. Apparently something more profound than tax aversion and tax incentives is generating a greater predilection for philanthropy. This more profound factor, we believe is at least in part a growing public culture and personal spirituality of care.

My translation of that academic language is that the wealthiest generation on the face of the earth wants to do more with its money than just pass it on to its offspring. It wants to see some of it being used for worthwhile social purposes. People do not behave charitably for tax purposes alone (something all experienced fund raisers already knew). Good professional advisors will recognize and encourage this widespread philanthropic desire—and smart not-for-profit organizations will do everything in their power to help them.

In an earlier chapter I described the Talmudic observation that people who encourage others to be generous are doubly blessed. Hardly a cocktail party or other social event occurs without someone telling an unflattering joke about lawyers. Some of them probably are well deserved. Yet, the history of philanthropy's growth in our nation is filled with wonderful, even heart-warming anecdotes about attorneys and other professional advisors—those men and women whose readiness to help clients exercise their charitable impulses in a tax-advantageous way led to the creation of new private foundations, new funds at community foundations, and new endowments for hospitals, universities, symphonies, and other institutions. We need more of those stories.

DISBURSING THE CHARITABLE DOLLAR

The foundation world is an arcane and mysterious realm for most people. When I write about foundations, I am referring to charitable institutions—usually with permanent endowments—whose primary purpose is to make grants to a range of not-for-profit organizations. Complicating matters, though, is the fact that anybody can use the word "foundation" to describe any kind of institution. Thus, for example, we have university and hospital foundations that exist simply to raise money for their respective organizations. And if you really want to get confused, keep in mind that grant makers categorize themselves as community foundations, corporate foundations, family foundations, health legacy foundations, independent foundations, and operating foundations.

"Organized philanthropy" is a phrase used to describe the work of these foundations. It is, of course, a bit of an oxymoron. Foundation giving is no more organized than any other human activity. Nonetheless, implied in descriptions of this institutionalized form of giving is that it calls for more deliberation and strategic thinking than our impulsive charitable decision to drop a buck in a Salvation Army kettle or even to write checks to the colleges from which we graduated. Many years ago, a marvelous cartoon about philanthropy appeared in *The New Yorker*. It depicted a young fellow in the office of a high rise building gleefully throwing handfuls of paper money out the window. Rushing toward him through the door from the hallway was an older gentleman with an expression of great alarm on his face. The caption reads something like this: "See here, young man, that's not exactly the way we do things here at The Ford Foundation."

According to The Foundation Center, the United States now is home to nearly 75,000 foundations. (That figure, by the way, has increased by 13,000 since I began work on this book.) In a speech I once gave, I described this exponentially growing phenomenon as the fascinating blend of capitalism, compound interest and compassion. Actually, there's a fourth "C" involved in the mix: Congress. Years ago our elected officials determined that it made sense to provide tax incentives which encourage individual and corporate generosity to establish organizations that exist, often in perpetuity, not to create financial profits but to be of service to society.

I've been associated with them for many years in varying kinds of relationships. I have worked for them, consulted with them, and conducted research on them. Recently I've been working with Jamil Zainaldin, the president of the Georgia Humanities Council, on a book about their history in the South. For 11 years I was the CEO of a membership organization of grant makers.

I have a great deal of affection and admiration for the people in organized philanthropy, but I also am a frequent critic of their work. That's because I believe that foundations play a vital role in our society, and I therefore want them to embody the highest principles of compassion, accountability, effectiveness, and courage.

Philanthropoids

Only a small percentage of U.S. foundations have paid staff. As a result, just a few thousand people in this country are actually employed to screen the millions of proposals they receive from not-for-profit organizations and recommend how their boards can best award tens of billions of dollars in grants. Since the resources for which they have stewardship responsibility do not belong to them, they are what Linus of *Peanuts* fame once said he'd like to be: a philanthropist with someone else's money. Decades ago some wag described this class of folk as "philanthropoids."

Day after day, month after month, year after year, their job is to sort through a never-ending avalanche of requests for support in search of those relatively few that fall within the foundation's guidelines and that demonstrate the likelihood of being able to deliver the results they promise.

Long ago I determined that I would not especially enjoy the responsibility of making those kinds of decisions. I suppose I could learn to say "no," but that kind of power would wreak havoc with my mental state. Here's what I predict would happen: after a long day of declining support to a lot of wonderful, caring, dedicated people who had persuasively pleaded their cases to me, I would like awake at night, trying to think of other ways to help them. I'm enough of an insomniac already; who needs that added grief? I've heard lots of people plaintively express their desire to work for a grant making foundation. Not me. My role model is Robin Hood. I'd much prefer to relieve the rich of their burdensome wealth and distribute it to the poor.

Everyone who has worked with or approached a philanthropoid for support will have an opinion on the subject of what constitutes a good foundation employee. For the purpose of this essay, I am going to make the assumption that such a person can perform routine duties like due-diligence investigations of prospective grantees. Instead, I have compiled my own list of preferred personal characteristics:

Humility

Everyone who enters the foundation world soon learns the old axiom about the fact that he or she will never again receive an honest evaluation of their work. Of course, that's not really true; most foundation executives and programs officers are evaluated by their boards or colleagues. But the old saw does correctly imply that grant seekers tend to be unduly respectful and even obsequious toward these gatekeepers who control access to philanthropic funds. Having this kind of power can lead these foundation employees to succumb to the belief that their positions somehow give them superior wisdom. If they believe that, they are fooling themselves. Most of the ones I know don't fall into this trap; they recognize that they must exercise their authority with a deep sense of humility.

Sensitivity

The executive of a Southeastern Council of Foundations' member had advertised for a new program officer. When I saw her at a reception, I asked what sort of person she was looking for. Her immediate response was, "Someone who's had to ask for money." I wholeheartedly agree. To be sure, there are some very gifted grant makers who have never worked the grant-seeking side of the street; never had to curry the favor of foundations and other donors. Nonetheless, in general, those who have had the experience, like Blanche duBois, of being "dependent upon the kindness of strangers," are often most likely to be receptive listeners and helpful philanthropoids, and to understand the awkwardness of the unequal footing on which grant makers and grant seekers stand. Those who haven't should work doubly hard at developing this sensitivity. One way to do that is to remind themselves daily that the success of their foundations' missions is totally dependent upon the effectiveness of their not-for-profit partners. To use a Zen-like metaphor, the superior foundation officers never forget that without the existence of strong not-for-profit organizations, philanthropy is the sound of one hand clapping.

Kindness

Thirty years ago, early in my fund raising career, my search for foundation funds brought me to an interview with a program officer of a foundation in Pittsburgh. I was ushered into his office and seated facing him across an enormous desk. The seemingly calculated placement of my chair assured that I was staring directly into the glare through the window behind him. From my vantage point he was a featureless silhouette. The purpose of my visit was simply to acquaint him with Clark College and its programs and to explore whether his foundation might entertain a proposal from us. I began the discussion by saying with what I thought was a warm and ingratiating tone, "I'm not here to ask for money today." His instantaneous response, fired back with a very cold inflection, was "Why not? That's your job, isn't it?" The remaining brief conversation went straight to hell. I'm relieved to be able to report that during the intervening years I have met only seven foundation officers who seem to have been hired specifically because of their innate malevolence.

Knowledge

The most helpful foundation representatives I have encountered are highly informed about the field for which they have responsibility. If they work for a general purpose foundation, they know a great deal about the not-for-profit sector in the geographical service area where they make grants. If they have responsibility for a specific program area like education, health, or the arts, they are very knowledgeable about which not-for-profits are operating in these spheres and about their best practices. As a result, they have gauges against which to evaluate requests for support and even suggestions about ways in which to improve proposals.

Entrepreneurship

Bill Somerville, the CEO of the Philanthropic Ventures Foundation and the iconoclastic author of *Grassroots Philanthropy* contends that every foundation officer should spend one-third of his/her time outside the office getting to know the community and looking for strong programs to fund. He doesn't believe in sitting behind his desk and waiting for proposals to arrive. Whether or not you agree with his thesis, it is true that the outstanding foundation folks I have known are always hungry for good ideas that will increase the positive impact of their grant making.

Passion

Great foundation officers like Bill Somerville also deeply love their work. They are grateful that fate has put them in a position to exercise stewardship over charitable resources. They rejoice at having strong not-for-profit and other funding partners. Above all, they are passionate about the opportunity to play a part in building stronger communities and a better world.

How did the folks who have these gifts—and there are many of them—acquire the tools to be good grant makers? The fact of the matter is that they either had them when they joined the field or they learned them on the job. Over the years I have known foundation employees who once were attorneys, bankers, college development officers, doctors, elected officials, journalists, military officers, social workers, and teachers.

Unlike other professions, grant makers essentially have no systematic program of formal education, internships, and residencies available to them. To be sure, they have the opportunity—should they choose to avail themselves of it—to attend the many fine workshops and conferences sponsored by national and regional associations of grant makers. But there clearly is no well defined career path by which to enter the field.

The situation is slowly changing as new training programs and academic curricula, like The Grantmaking School at Grand Valley (MI) State University come into existence. It needs to change, because we are starting to witness the retirement of some of the most able grant makers in the country—even as the number of foundations radically increases and the scrutiny of the field intensifies. I hope that more foundations will assume responsibility for funding programs that will encourage young people as well as second-career people to consider foundation work as a profession and then to equip them for that work.

Ten Commandments for Foundation Board Members

About four years ago I was asked to speak to the board of a foundation that had acquired significant new assets and was contemplating an expanded program of grant making. It is the only foundation of any appreciable size in its part of the state, so both its challenges and opportunities are great.

Since I've made more than a few of these presentations over the years, I threw one of the set pieces that I had delivered before into my briefcase, and drove four hours along mostly rural back roads to the small town in which the foundation is located. After a very pleasant dinner with the executive director, I retired for the night in the town's only decent motel.

When I woke early the next morning and looked over my speech notes, I felt compelled to compose something different. As dawn broke, my yellow legal pad was filled with several pages of recommendations for the board members to whom I would be speaking. When I counted them up, I realized that, quite by accident, I had come up with a set of Ten Commandments. It just worked out that way. I could as easily have written eight or 11 or 27. (Remember the famous scene in Mel Brooks' *History of the World, Part I*, when Moses comes down from Mount Sinai with three tablets, and proclaims, "I bring you 15—(at which point he drops one of them and quickly amends his announcement)—10 commandments"? Anyway, here they are:

I.

Thou shalt not forget that it is not thy money.

Yes, the assets over which you exercise stewardship are indeed private resources, but they have been set aside in trust for the public good. Determining just what the public good might be is one of your primary responsibilities—one that is worthy of very thoughtful deliberation and, therefore, one that you dare not take lightly.

II.

Thou shalt not be arrogant.

One of the cardinal sins to which all philanthropists and philanthropoids are subject is *hubris*. Because you are stewards of wealth, people now will laugh at all your jokes. More significantly, it will be very hard to get an honest assessment of your performance. These kinds of conditions make it easy to succumb to the assumption that you're doing a great job. Assiduously practice the virtue of humility.

III.

Thou shalt not confuse the foundation's importance with thy personal worth.

As a board member, you can expect to be approached in grocery store lines, at Rotary meetings, and after services at your church or synagogue by friends and associates who want you to use your influence on behalf of not-for-profit organizations they represent. Resist the impulse to act like Lord or Lady Bountiful by telling them that you're willing to put in a supportive word for them. Keep your distance from them by informing them politely to submit an application like everyone else and take their chances. If they get too close, you might even be guilty of a conflict of interest. (See Commandment IV) Furthermore, do not let your foundation's grantmaking be a substitute for your personal generosity.

IV.

Thou shalt shun all conflicts of interest.

Is there anyone on a foundation board who hasn't learned that board members are not permitted to derive personal gain from their position? Make sure your foundation has policies against conflicts of interest and regularly applies them to everything you do. Even then, and even though you are completely aboveboard, some people still will suspect the worst of you. A scrupulously honest friend who is the vice president of a foundation in our region put a new roof on his house and bought a new car about the same time. Some members of the community still are willing to suspect that his involvement with the foundation made it possible. We can joke about this story, because he is an intensely ethical person, but the fact remains that you must do all in your power to position yourself beyond reproach.

V.

Thou shalt make information about thy foundation readily accessible.

If foundations ever were able to hide the details of what they do, the internet has rendered that possibility a thing of the past. People who believe that keeping things secret will make it harder for others to ask them for money are living in a dream world. Regularly publish all relevant financial data about your investments and your grant making in the newspaper, in an annual report, or on your website. And by all means, also keep impeccable records of all that you do.

VI.

Thou shalt follow the discipline of professional development.

It's assumed that among the reasons you serve on a foundation board are your possession of a modicum of concern for your fellow human beings and an adequate IQ. Nonetheless, although governing a foundation does not require that you be Albert Schweitzer or a member of MENSA, it does call upon skills that can be developed and honed. Make it a point to attend conferences, workshops, and other events to stay current on the laws that regulate your work, to learn about grant making success stories from other foundations and other good practices, and to discover new community needs in the area you serve.

VII.

Thou shalt lead.

Foundation work is not just about the money. You and your board colleagues do not just have to sit passively and wait for proposals to arrive through the mail or over the transom. You have the clout to convene your grant making peers to discuss common community challenges and to bring together not-for-profit leaders to learn about their concerns.

VIII.

Thou shalt respect and strengthen the rest of the not-for-profit sector.

The agencies and organizations through which you route your grants are essential to your success. It behooves you to help them function as effectively and efficiently as possible, to treat them with kindness and courtesy, and to look for ways to strengthen their effectiveness.

IX.

Thou shalt evaluate thyself.

Subject all that you do to regular scrutiny. Grade yourself and your colleagues on your governance. Invite your grant seekers to rate your helpfulness to them—even if you didn't give them a dime (perhaps especially if you didn't give them a dime). Look for ways to measure with sensitivity the impact of your giving.

X.

Thou shalt promote the creation of new philanthropy.

Even though foundation grant making can never take the place of public funding, we still need more private sector giving. Encourage your friends to start family foundations or funds at community foundations. Provide seed money to launch a community foundation if none exists in your area. Make challenge grants to encourage the formation of giving circles and other philanthropic consortia. Support programs that engage high school students in the knowledge and practice of philanthropy.

Okay, I know that it's not exactly Holy Writ, but the willingness of board members to be guided by these maxims may serve them well and even help them to identify other pointers that I failed to include.

Georges Clemenceau, France's prime minister during the early part of the 20th century, declared that the conduct of war was too important to be left only to generals. In similar fashion, philanthropy is too significant an enterprise to be directed by CEOs alone. Service as a foundation board member is a noble vocation.

What Price Stewardship?

On many days I am able to rhapsodize about the great work done by foundations as they seek to repair the world. Nonetheless, I believe that their performance and the public perception of their value to society could be dangerously undercut by those engaged in the practice of compensating their "volunteer" board members.

Apparently not everyone shares my concern. A recent study proudly declared that 66% of the 10,000 largest foundations in the country don't pay their trustees a dime. That's fine, but according to my arithmetic, it also means that 34% of them do. Furthermore the study leaves unexamined another 60,000+ foundations.

One of the reasons for this study is that Congress—not for the first time in history—has been taking a harder look at the way foundations and other not-for-profit organizations conduct their affairs. Our elected officials were moved to do so in part by a series of newspaper exposés that threw the spotlight on cases in which board members were receiving what seemed to be egregiously high compensation—in some cases more than they were disbursing in grants!

Organized philanthropy's leaders were quick to respond that these abuses of privilege by some were exceptions to the norm. However, the fact of the matter is that we don't really know how widespread the abuses might be. The field is still relatively unaudited, and tens of thousands of foundations do not voluntarily divulge much information about themselves. What we do know is that some foundations routinely compensate their board members and that some of those compensation levels are, by any reasonable standards, rather high. (Please note that I certainly have no objection to reimbursing foundation board members for travel to their meetings or even to conferences to further their professional development. I further support the payment of reasonable and competitive fees to attorneys, accountants, and other professionals on the board who perform valued services to the foundation.)

Those foundations that pay their board members have a variety of justifications for doing so, including the wishes of the founding donors.

Many of them revolve around the value of the time that board members devote to their work. In response to that contention, I decided to do some rough calculations. I generously assumed that those board members met monthly (probably for at least three hours at a time). Then I made the further assumption that they attended six committee meetings a year, each of which lasted three hours. That's a total of 54 hours a year for each board member—in other words, a week's worth of work for many salaried working stiffs. What's that worth? $750? $1,000? Well, some foundations are shelling out anywhere from $20,000 to $200,000 for these services. Divide 54 into any of those figures, and you wind up with a very nice hourly wage rate. Furthermore, many of those being compensated (the report I cited above identifies 7,132 individuals) already have well-paid jobs or comfortable retirement incomes.

Let me be clear. There is currently nothing illegal about paying board members for their services, although I don't know of any foundation which would make a grant to a not-for-profit organization that compensated its board members. The only guideline offered by the IRS is that foundation expenses be reasonable. And giving away philanthropic dollars is certainly an awesome responsibility—one that I am sure the vast majority of paid board members take very seriously.

However, would it be churlish to note that very few of them who have this rare opportunity have received professional training in the art of charitable disbursement? One could also reasonably question whether they have otherwise demonstrated a level of discernment significantly greater than that of their fellow human beings. Yet they are receiving special compensation for making the same kind of humanitarian judgments that all of us do when we decide which checks we are going to write for charitable purposes. Our checks may have fewer zeroes to the left of the decimal point, but writing them requires the same basic judgment skills. Some solicitations will receive more, some less, and some none.

Ultimately, though, since foundations, by law, operate in the public trust, the fundamental question may possibly be not how much payment these individuals should receive, but whether they should receive any compensation at all. Canadian law does not permit foundations to pay their board members, and the wisdom of their grant making doesn't seem to be impaired by this restriction.

In fairness, it should be noted that a relatively small number of foundations make important efforts to recruit community leaders from lower down the economic scale to serve on their boards. They claim that these individuals are sacrificing valuable time when they could be earning a living to participate in governance and grant making. If that's really the case (although I think most of those folks would be honored to serve without compensation), then I'm not going to be a zealot on the subject. Go ahead and pay them a modest amount; Pablo Eisenberg, a frequent critic of board compensation, has suggested a cap of $8,000 per year.

The opportunity to be a steward of resources that have been set aside for the public good should be one of those pinnacle moments of great citizenship. It is a privilege to be asked to serve on the board of any grant making foundation, and that privilege itself should be sufficient compensation.

Foundations now paying their board members are not likely to cease and desist or even to reduce the remuneration levels voluntarily on the strength of reading my opinion. However, they may not have to take that step. Legislators and regulators could make the decision for them and in the process call into further question the value of all philanthropic institutions. During a period when foundations are under scrutiny, anything that undermines public confidence in foundations is a threat to the trust that is one of the field's most important assets.

When I showed this essay to my wife, she asked me what I would do if asked to serve as a well-compensated foundation trustee. My initial response was to paraphrase Mark Twain. He once noted that although he was not particularly fond of millionaires, it would be dangerous to offer him the position. For all of my bold assertions, I can only hope that I'd have the guts to decline that kind of offer or at least the paycheck that came with it.

Seeing the World through New Lenses

During my 40 years of traversing the not-for-profit sector, I've witnessed a lot of change. One of the most positive developments has been the growing diversity and inclusiveness in the field of philanthropy.

As you've already read, I first stumbled into this line of work by taking a job as a program officer at an operating foundation. In those days the foundation field and corporate giving programs were dominated—with a handful of notable exceptions—by a fraternity of older white heterosexual men. They were sincere people who for the most part cared deeply about what they were doing and worked hard to make the world a better place. They (and I) often had a clearly defined sense of what needed to be done. Unfortunately, our criteria for a better society were shaped almost entirely by our own experiences. We had precious little understanding of the real needs and sensitivities of women and people of color and certainly not of folks with different sexual orientations than our own.

Fortunately for all of us, the spirit of the Civil Rights Movement emboldened other disenfranchised populations to begin pushing for a greater say in their own lives and a place in the decision-making that affected them. The early pioneers had to work hard to prove themselves. However, as some women were fond of reciting, "Whatever we do we must do twice as well as men to be thought half as good. Luckily this is not difficult."

These "newcomers" to our field, like the veterans, have included their share of incompetents and frauds too. But the encouraging news is that the increase in sheer numbers of non-white, non-straight, non-males has given us the opportunity to do a much better job of judging people on their merits alone and increased our sensitivity to the needs of our communities.

I have truly been blessed by my professional association with an admirable collection of leaders who are women, people of color and/or gay. (Having been married to a couple of feminists and being the father of two women with a strong sense of their identity has obviously helped to alter my perceptions of reality too.) Don't get me wrong: some of my best friends continue to be straight white men. However, few of them could have helped me to see our world through the lenses of colleagues who know what it is like not to be born into a sense of entitlement.

During my years as a consultant, I remember an occasion when a client's board members and I were discussing whom we should involve in the discussion of a proposed new program. One young matron on the board, who had not been especially vocal during the conversation, quietly noted, "You know, I don't think you ever go wrong if you err on the side of inclusiveness." I have been deeply influenced by that powerful line and quoted it frequently.

In brief, then, I am a passionate and profound believer in diversity and have been so most of my life. It's a core value that I try to affirm in everything I do personally and professionally. Conversely, I feel extremely uncomfortable when I am trapped in any gathering of people who all look and sound like me. I may happen to have an affection for all of the other individuals in the room with white complexions, dark suits, and red ties, but taken collectively they can be decidedly uninteresting. Staring at mirror images of yourself doesn't yield a whole lot of new insight.

The roots of my feelings are complex and varied, and I'm not going to delve deeply into them here. Suffice it to say that the strength of my commitment to diversity was firmly cemented in place by the rare opportunity to serve on the staff of a black church in Harlem for a year back in 1964 and to spend several years as the single white administrator at historically black Clark College in Atlanta and then the Atlanta University Center during the 1960s and 70s.

It is a matter of fact that the philanthropic realm has become a lot more inclusive since the 1960s. Has it come far enough? Not by a long shot, especially at the board level, and definitely not in the eyes of individuals and organizations that now are working to legislate greater inclusiveness.

Although it may sound contradictory, I oppose that step. What we have is not a situation of racially or otherwise exclusive public policy that needs to be overturned by corrective legislation. No foundation of which I'm aware has a stated policy that forbids the election of women, people of color, or gays and lesbians to its board. The attempt to impose a uniform standard of diversity upon even some of the 75,000 foundations in the United States is ill-conceived, probably unenforceable, and perhaps even illegal.

The best argument for greater diversity has nothing to do with political correctness. It is an essentially functional one. To the extent that a foundation wishes to be responsive to the challenge of serving the public good, it enhances its understanding and sensitivity to the community it serves by drawing upon a variety of insights and experiences from that community. Diversity is a source of information, and good grant making can only benefit from its rich and varied store.

So how does a foundation become more diverse? Of late the field has been sponsoring a wide range of consultations, workshops, and studies to answer what seems to me to be a fairly simple question. I am reminded of the establishment of the Community Foundation for the Fox Valley Region in Appleton, Wisconsin, to which I provided some consultation back in 1987. When the city's leaders (all white males) convened to explore how best to get started, one of the first questions had to do with who would serve on the board. Everyone they could think of, including themselves, already had their plates full with other civic commitments. One of the younger men in the room suggested "Why don't we advertise?" His recommendation may have been semi-facetious, but the idea gained traction. The foundation placed an ad in the local newspaper, inviting applications and nominations for board service. More than 200 individuals, many of them women, surfaced. Clearly, leadership was not in such short supply as originally thought.

Foundations have the responsibility, whether or not they continue under scrutiny or face other challenges to their important independence, to continue giving leadership to the promotion of greater diversity, to model it in their own organizations, and to document the ways in which it does improve their grant making. Nothing else they may do will contribute more greatly to the strength of our sector and the building of—as the Mary Reynolds Babcock Foundation puts it—just and caring communities.

Committed to Change

Emmett Carson, the CEO and President of the Silicon Valley Community Foundation, inspired these next reflections. Several years ago Emmett and I both were scheduled to deliver presentations to an assembly of grant makers in Alabama. After I spoke about the importance of ethical accountability, Emmett delivered a speech about how foundations could best support advocacy.

The subject of advocacy is a touchy one. It is, of course, correct that foundations themselves cannot lobby for specific legislation unless it is in "self-defense." In other words, they can raise all the fuss they want if proposed laws threaten the way in which they do their work. However, although the nuances of regulations that address the lobbying issue are not especially difficult to grasp and although it is well documented that they can indeed support organizations that lobby for legislative change, many of them shy away from this kind of assertive grant making. One of the reasons for their reluctance is that their attorneys—quite incorrectly—have told them that they can't do it. As a result, some of them even explicitly state in their guidelines that they will not provide support to not-for-profits that lobby.

Emmett, however, came up with a most creative way to engage his audience in the subject. He began by posing a question to the foundation representatives in the room. "How many of your organizations," he asked "have mission statements that declare they exist to preserve the status quo?" Not surprisingly, no one raised a hand.

"All right," he went on, "how many of your foundations have something in your mission statements that makes a reference to the betterment/change/transformation of your community or society or claims to be interested in the eradication of a particular social problem?" Hands shot up all over the room.

"Well, then," said Emmett, "Why aren't you supporting advocacy by not-for-profit organizations to amend or improve legislation and public policy that will bring about that kind of essential change?" His listeners sat mute as they pondered this possible contradiction. He continued to remind them that he was not preaching to them—simply inviting them to be true to their own purposes. It was a powerful attention-getter.

I wish we had an audiotape of Emmett's remarks, because I think they should be required listening for every member of the foundation world. What he had to say was, in effect, an exposition of a parable that I have seen in varied forms. Here's one simplified version of it:

> Some people who live beside a river at the foot of a raging cataract notice that a growing number of men, women, and children are being swept over the waterfall and badly hurt as they are hurled onto the rocks below. After thoughtful consideration, the concerned citizens who have been rescuing these victims from the river decide that they need to build a hospital to care for their injured fellow creatures. They raise the necessary funds for the facility and staff it with competent personnel who provide excellent medical treatment—but badly hurt people continue to appear in the river at ever-increasing rates, putting enormous strains on the hospital and its staff. Finally, one day a wise leader in the community offers a suggestion, "Instead of continuing to minister to these injured people," she says, "why don't we try a different approach? There's an organization that has been trying for years to get the state to build a dam that will keep people from being pulled over the waterfall. Perhaps we need to be supporting its efforts?

For many years, Central Presbyterian Church in Atlanta, the downtown congregation to which I belong, conducted an outreach ministry for homeless people. Through it we sought to alleviate some of the miseries that are the crippling by-products of living on the streets of the city. However, we eventually came to the realization that our well-meaning efforts were doing little more than slapping bandages on symptoms of larger problems—like the lack of sufficient rehabilitation centers for the men and women who suffered from substance addiction; the absence of sufficient homes for the mentally ill; and the paucity of affordable housing for the working poor. That realization led to the expansion of our work through the formation of an advocacy program that now lobbies for changes in legislation that will provide those kinds of services. We continue daily to bandage the "wounds" of homelessness—a great way to keep us in touch with the needs that surround us—but we also are trying to change the systems that contribute to the wounding.

This dilemma faces many foundations as well. They daily are offered opportunities to support not-for-profit organizations that are struggling to cope with the challenge of meeting the immediate needs of victims of addiction, abuse, poor health, insufficient education, and other damage. However, they also have the opportunity to invest in organizations that are working to change the laws and systems that exacerbate and even contribute to these conditions.

Of course, there is no single correct answer to the question of how foundations should respond. The important thing to remember is that they have a choice about whether to make an immediate or a lasting difference. For further consideration about the choices that foundations face, you may want to turn to the next essays.

Five Loaves of Bread and Two Fish

Two stories will serve to introduce this essay:

1.   A small group was sitting around a table in a classroom at our church. We were discussing what we could do to expand our ministry to the homeless. With us that evening as a guest was a friend of mine, the Rev. Eduard Loring. A quarter of a century ago, he and his wife, Murphy Davis, founded the Open Door Community to care for people who live in the street. Ed is a prophetic figure, and, like all prophets, he can be a royal pain in the butt, because he makes our consciences squirm.

At some point, without giving the matter a great deal of thought, I opined that we did, after all, have only limited resources. Ed immediately jumped on me like a flea on a dog. In no uncertain terms, he reminded me that our deficit was not one of resources but of commitment and will. And, of course, he was right. Nobody like Bill Gates belongs to our congregation, but everyone in the room and virtually all of our fellow parishioners lead comfortable lives, are surrounded by lots of material possessions, and have never been forced to go without a meal. I have never forgotten the lesson I learned that night.

2.   A roomful of foundation executives and board members from the Atlanta metropolitan area had gathered for their quarterly luncheon. The program consisted of an overview of the major fund raising campaigns that they could expect to be asked to support during the coming year or so. We heard about drives for expensive projects like the new symphony hall, a proposed green beltway around the city. and the children's wing of the downtown hospital.

Then, during the question and answer period, several of the folks in the room began to raise the issue of the many other not-for-profits that needed financial help. However, what might have been an interesting discussion came to a crashing conclusion when a veteran grant maker pontificated, "You've got to remember that we have only limited resources." Because I am not Ed Loring, I held my tongue, but something in me wished he had been present.

Parker Palmer (a classmate during my first year in seminary and one of my favorite writers and thinkers) has some useful observations on this subject. In an article entitled, "Scarcity, Abundance and the Gift of Community," Palmer notes that our country is blessed with great abundance. And yet, as he points out, the world tends to operate on the assumption of scarcity. Our standard economics textbooks, he has noted, begin with the explicitly stated principle that the primary problem of every economy is scarce resources. He then writes:

> We see scarcity being created everywhere. Our schools act as if intelligence is scarce, as if there is not enough to go around; or as if there is only one kind of intelligence, and it alone merits rewards. Some churches act as if salvation is scarce, as if only the right formula or certain behavior earns salvation. Our professions act as if there are not enough human resources to go around. The healing professions sometimes encourage people to assume that affirmation and esteem are in short supply and must be purchased from experts. Most institutions act as if power is scarce and should be put into the hands of only a few. Shared power is not on their agenda.

Palmer goes on to recount the well known story from the New Testament that describes the miracle of Jesus feeding five thousand hungry people. As he explains, the images of hunger and food are both literal and metaphorical images of the relationship between scarcity and abundance. No one understands exactly what happened that day, but we do know that it all began when a small boy announced his willingness to share his meal of five small loaves of bread and two fish. It is quite possible that his generous spirit inspired others to follow his lead.

For many years—and I know that I'm overstating the point—the standard practice for beginning to address a poor community's needs was to catalog its pathologies and then to throw money at them. Then along came John McKnight and Jody Kretzmann at Northwestern University with one of the most transformational shifts to hit the not-for-profit world in the 20th century. They put forward the revolutionary notion that positive change can best occur in distressed areas when people start building upon the individual and organizational strengths and capabilities in their neighborhoods and communities. In what they called "Asset-Based Community Development" (and, in a way, it was as simple as ABCD), they showed folks how to map those assets and build upon them. It's a great example of how seeing the world through the lens of abundance can always trump a perspective that is limited to perceiving only scarcity. To return to the New Testament story for one more moment, instead of conducting a needs analysis, Jesus instead asked his disciples to do a survey of existing assets. That survey turned up the kid with the bread and fish, and the rest, as they say, is history.

Some years ago, I attended a conference in Washington that focused upon the topic of creating new philanthropic resources. It was and is a subject dear to my heart because the South still has a deficit of permanent charitable resources. Our region will soon be home to one-third of the nation's population, but we also must lay claim to being the location for more than 40% of the poverty in America. Yet the assets of Southern foundations constitute only 11% of the country's philanthropic capital. Hardest hit by this pattern of disparity is the rural South. Only a tiny percentage of the grant making by these foundations goes to rural areas.

There continues to be an enormous need for more urban dollars to flow to rural areas. However, sometime during the conference and on the way back to Atlanta, my thinking turned in a new direction. I began to muse about a concept that I found myself describing as a "philanthropy index." Surely, I reasoned, there ought to be a way to calculate the potential in so-called poor, rural communities for building their own charitable endowments. (I didn't recognize or acknowledge it at the time, but that McKnight-Kretzmann way of thinking must have been influencing my thought processes.)

I am not a research scholar and I tend to use statistics the way a drunk uses a lamp post—more for support than for illumination. Fortunately, though, I have some very smart colleagues. I challenged them—and was able to sweeten the pot with a grant we were able to obtain—to come up with a set of publicly available indicators that would measure a rural community's philanthropic potential.

They eventually identified 12 of them. The list included measures like the presence of grant making foundations and not-for-profit organizations; levels of charitable giving; work-force stability; household incomes; and, very important, the existence of "social capital" (those formal and informal networks that promote relationships in a community). We next field-tested *The Philanthropy Index for Small Towns and Rural Areas of the South*. It was exciting to watch as, figuratively speaking, the light bulbs went on above the heads of the local groups with which we worked when they realized that their communities were not as poor as (and sometimes much wealthier than) they may have imagined. Furthermore, that very change in self-awareness became a motivational tool to begin thinking about how best to build a pool of philanthropic assets for their communities.

Even as were working on our *Philanthropy Index*, Jeff Yost and his colleagues at the Nebraska Community Foundation launched a parallel effort. Inspired by the research of Paul Schervish and John Havens about the intergenerational transfer of wealth, the Nebraska folks calculated the potential worth of household estates and used those figures to launch a campaign that encourages individuals to set aside a percentage of those estates for charitable purposes.

Both of these efforts were part of a larger initiative called New Ventures in Giving that was directed by the Forum of Regional Associations of Grantmakers. New Ventures embraced and supported a collection of programs, like the formation of giving circles, that sought to stimulate charitable asset building and giving by individuals and associations around the country who don't fit into the traditional framework of organized philanthropy. All of these examples are strong illustrations of how seeming scarcity can be translated into abundance. The national funders who underwrote New Ventures deserve praise for embracing a vision of promoting increased philanthropy.

At the beginning of this century, when the go-go economy of the 1990s suddenly changed direction and began going into the toilet (not unlike the situation we're in once again), a survey of foundations revealed that most of them were feeling "poor." We're the richest country on earth, and foundation assets, despite the shrinkages in their portfolios, still were enormous. (Come on, where is it etched in stone that you can always expect a 30% annual return on investment?). Nonetheless, lots of people in the world of philanthropy were walking around with scowls on their faces as if they'd gone bankrupt. I guess it's all relative. During this same period, I'm told, the board members of one family foundation became terribly distressed to learn that the company whose wealth had created the foundation was going to have to sell its second airplane—thereby forcing them to travel on commercial carriers.

We Americans pride ourselves, with some justification, on our generosity, but the fact remains that we collectively still give away only about 2% of our income. Although there are notable exceptions, most of us are not committed to sacrificial giving. My mentor Irving Warner puts it more pithily: "Did you ever see anybody go broke by being generous?" St. Francis of Assisi is the only one I can think of.

I hope that a growing number of foundations and individuals will learn to view the world through a prism—and it doesn't have to be rose-colored—that permits them to see potential when everyone else sees problems. They should be leaders in embracing a vision of abundance and using their grant making to promote it.

The Public Good

While still the CEO of the Southeastern Council of Foundations, I tried to remain professionally neutral on the subject of what our members should support. Years ago this association intentionally threw up a very large tent under which all sorts of foundations and giving programs were welcome. SECF has a member that supports genealogical research and another that works to protect the bald eagle. One member only makes capital grants to colleges and universities. Others support programs to protect the environment, to promote social justice, and to empower the disenfranchised. A lot of others are general purpose foundations that are willing to consider a wide variety of proposals. All of these missions are laudable. I also was and remain convinced that it would be very ill-informed and even dangerous to take away the independence of any of our nation's private foundations.

In 2005, after the SECF board adopted a suggested set of guiding principles for these grant makers, we were field-testing them on a group of foundation representatives in Virginia. The first principle states simply, "We will serve the public good." It's one of those credal statements that are central to organized philanthropy. That commitment is the primary reason the federal government permits people to set aside endowment funds for charitable purposes without subjecting them to taxation. I wish, therefore, that every foundation board would periodically have a serious discussion about whether and how it is serving that public good.

I offer that modest suggestion, because one of the people in the room responded with a snort. "It sounds like the Boy Scout oath," he declared. In a sense, he was right. It does, at least on a first reading, seem to be a self-evident piece of puffery. However, as I suggested to him, its simplicity is deceptive.

To illustrate that point I told a story about the evening a year or so before that my wife and I went to see a performance of La Bohéme by the Atlanta Opera Company. We found our seats and began to read the program. Because I have never completely forgotten my years as a fund raiser, I immediately turned to the back of the booklet to study the list of patrons and donors. I was immediately impressed by the discovery that one of our city's foundations had contributed half a million dollars to the organization.

Nonetheless, no sooner had I mentally congratulated everyone involved in securing this grant than my thoughts turned in a very different direction. A few blocks from the auditorium in which Puccini's work was to be performed is a less-than-ideal shelter in which hundreds of homeless men crowd every night for a few hours of relief from their life on the streets. For me, at least, this dichotomy of need posed a dilemma. Does a major grant that makes it possible for a very small minority of the population to listen to an admittedly lovely musical soap opera in Italian constitute a proper response to the mandate of serving the public good or would those funds be more properly used to alleviate a major social problem?

Since that meeting in Virginia, I've thought of another more nuanced example to highlight the problematic determination of what constitutes the public good. The Atlanta Community Food Bank is a wonderful institution. Its founding director, Bill Bolling, is one of the most extraordinary not-for-profit executives I've ever known. He balances deep compassion with practical wisdom. Had he been so inclined, he could have been an equally effective for-profit CEO too.

A couple of years ago his organization, with justifiable pride, dedicated a new $11 million facility that rivals those of some major, commercial grocery chains. The Food Bank clearly has come a long way since Bill founded it in the basement of St. Luke's Episcopal Church many years ago. The many donors who contributed to its construction could feel a great measure of pride, too.

And yet, without meaning to sound overly judgmental, I think one could make the case that this support does not necessarily constitute great grant making. Leaving aside the obvious benefit of efficiently distributing affordable food to people who are hungry, this achievement might also be seen as the symbol of a larger failure: the lack of a collective will to eradicate the need for a food bank. Compassionate people, it could be argued, have essentially conceded that they are incapable of eliminating hunger in our wealthy city. Instead they have unwittingly helped to institutionalize hunger.

Foundations have done and continue to do many important things. One cannot walk through the heart of my city without seeing the impact of their generosity upon daily life: parks, university buildings, theaters and concert halls, as well as daycare centers homeless shelters and social service agencies of all kinds. As a result, those of us who already were destined to lead comfortable lives enjoy "better living through philanthropy," and those who struggle to survive receive a measure of relief. And yet, sometimes good can be the enemy of the best.

Even though I recommend regular and vigorous discussion about what constitutes the public good, sometimes I also wonder whether we're guilty of over-analysis. Perhaps we should declare a moratorium on studies to determine what needs to be done. Maybe it's time instead to pool the resources of our not-for-profit organizations and foundations to do what we already know works.

The studies I have read make clear that:

- Infants who are cuddled three times a day are much more likely to succeed in life than those who don't receive this early affirmation of love.

- What happens to children before they are two years old has more to do with determining what kind of adults they will be than all the education we later try to provide them.

- High school dropouts are twice as likely to wind up in prison as smokers are to get lung cancer.

- Adult mentoring has one of the most positive effects on the future of young people.

Many years ago I wrote a letter to our local community foundation in which I made this recommendation: give leadership to a city-wide effort to make sure that all children born in the local charity hospital are guaranteed a regimen of cuddling followed by pre-school nurturing and health care. As they grow older, make certain that they are assured of a series of adult mentors until they graduate from high school.

An initiative of this kind would require a lot of coordinated work over a long period of time. Some not-for-profits wouldn't receive foundation funding unless they were contributing to the success of the program. Other foundations would have to become partners in this effort. Would it produce results? I'm convinced that it would.

As I have wrestled in my own mind with the issue of what constitutes the public good, I have been greatly taken with the wisdom of Maimonides. For those not familiar with him, Maimonides (Moshe ben Maimon) was a rabbi and philosopher who lived and worked in Andalusia, Morocco, and Egypt. He also was considered by many to be the greatest physician of his time. Born in the 1130s, his works on Jewish law and ethics met with opposition during his lifetime, but he was posthumously acknowledged to be one of the foremost rabbinical arbiters and philosophers in Jewish history. His *Mishneh Torah* today retains canonical authority as a codification of Talmudic law.

In that work he postulated what he called the Laws of Charity. One translation of the first and highest level states:

> The greatest level, above which there is no greater, is to support a fellow Jew by endowing him with a gift or loan, or entering into a partnership with him, or finding employment for him, in order to strengthen his hand until he need no longer be dependent upon others...

During the past year I have threaded this admonition from Maimonides through a lot of my writing and speaking. One of the fascinating discoveries has been that it resonates well with audience members who are both so-called conservatives and so-called liberals. Political allegiances don't seem to get in the way of appreciating the notion that the highest form of philanthropy might involve moving the recipients of generosity from a position of dependency to one of self-sufficiency.

I happen to believe that Maimonides' top priority sets the ultimate standard, but there is, of course, no single correct answer to the question of what constitutes the public good. However, the question is the core issue for all philanthropy and the process of looking for the answer may be almost as important as the results.

The Future of Foundations

Barring a seismic shift in attitudes or public policy, thousands more foundations (as well as funds at community foundations) will continue to come into existence during the next several decades. The intergenerational transfer of wealth is alive and well.

Among the challenges they face will be the need to find a large cadre of CEOs and staff members to replace a generation of leaders that is stepping off the scene. I suspect that a parallel effort may well involve the establishment of more formal training mechanisms to prepare men and women for careers in the world of organized philanthropy. We also are going to see the continued emergence of an entire industry of specialized professional advisors whose legal, accounting, investment, and other skills will be focused upon assisting these foundations with governance, management, and financial affairs. I know we will see the formation of more geographically focused donor groups, and I hope we also will see greater coordination among their national and regional associations. In short, philanthropy will continue to be a growth industry.

These foundations, especially the largest ones, will continue to wrestle with the issue of how to be more focused and strategic about their grant making as they seek to achieve the greatest positive impact with the resources at their disposal.

I further would like to believe that foundations will practice greater collaboration—something they often demand of grant seekers but are reluctant to impose upon themselves. Because of the growing resources at their disposal, they truly could bring about significant change. In two of the Southern states, the sale of not-for-profit hospitals to for-profit companies has led to the formation of private foundations with combined assets of more than one billion dollars. However, only two of these foundations make grants on a state-wide basis. The rest restrict their giving much more narrowly, usually to the service areas of the hospitals from whose sales they were created. All of them are doing valuable and important work. Nonetheless, it's exciting to imagine what might be possible if they combined not only their assets but the lessons they have learned from their grant making experiences to tackle jointly some of the challenges that face the entire population of their states.

I'm idealistic, but I'm not naïve. I know that collaboration is messy and difficult; I think it was Jocelyn Elder, the former U.S. Surgeon General, who described collaboration as an unnatural act performed by non-consenting adults. But I continue to live in hope that these and other foundations everywhere will find ways to perform that act.

However, the most formidable challenge that foundations are likely to face involves continued legislative and public scrutiny. In 2004, the U.S. Senate Finance Committee declared war on foundations and other institutions in the not-for-profit sector. The impetus for these hostilities, sad to say, was some egregious and widely-publicized misbehavior by foundations and large not-for-profits who had squandered their resources on excessive compensation and perks for executive officers and board members.

The Finance Committee went on the attack. Its first salvo was an 18-page, single-spaced diatribe against the sector. Despite the fact that ample legislation already existed to keep it in line, the committee initially contemplated the passage of new and even more restrictive laws. To its way of thinking, the same kind of arrogance and greed that had led to the passage of the Sarbanes-Oxley legislation to curb for-profit companies now needed to be directed at the not-for-profits.

As the previously cited Edward Queen has reminded me, there is precedent for this kind of Congressional animosity. Thomas Jefferson had serious misgivings about the concentration of great wealth in the hands of a few people and didn't really like corporations of any kind. Consequently, in the 1700s, he and his landed gentry pals successfully forced the liquidation of an Episcopal Church trust and the distribution of its funds to the poor and needy of Virginia's counties. Since then and throughout our country's history, there have been regularly recurring efforts, usually led by Populists from the South and Midwest, to regulate foundations ever more tightly and even to force them to liquidate all of their assets. All foundations and other not-for-profits are now profoundly aware that they need to do a much better job of taking even more seriously the need to be both legally compliant and ethically accountable.

However, in the wake of what was a relatively frantic period of accusations, rebuttals, public hearings, lobbying, and debate, we now are witnessing a new surge of challenges to the right of foundations to support what they choose. Proposed new legislation in several states would require the largest foundations to document that their philanthropic activity is focused upon organizations that exist to help our country's neediest citizens.

Perhaps I'm being cynical, but I don't think that these efforts are being motivated by an especially altruistic vision. Rather, I believe that a major reason for some lawmakers to covet more control over philanthropic capital has to do with the amount of money involved. The field is fond of saying that philanthropy is about much more than the money. That's true, of course, but the trillions of dollars that Paul Schervish of Boston College has predicted will be involved (a transfer which seems to be happening at an even faster rate than he once imagined) is beginning to attract the attention of public officials.

Why? Because even as the first wave of those estimated trillions of dollars is gushing into charitable reserves, our federal and state governments are posting record deficits and, according to some critics, demonstrating no political will to raise taxes from those best able to pay them. Essential services are being cut. As a result, it seems inevitable to me that we are going to hear more demands for foundation resources to provide those safety nets that governments no longer are supplying.

Never mind that philanthropic dollars—even all of our newfound wealth—pales into insignificance when compared with public treasuries. As I have noted elsewhere, it is a ridiculous contention that private giving by both individuals and foundations can replace the public dollars and new public policies that are required to ensure that all Americans receive adequate education and health care. For all of their seeming great wealth, the assets of foundations don't even show up on the radar screen when compared with public resources. If all of the foundations in the United States were to liquidate their nearly half a trillion dollars in assets today, the total would barely cover the interest payment on the federal deficit.

It remains to be seen whether these calls for foundation help will ripen into new legislation that seeks to tell foundations which organizations they should support or whether they will simply lead to higher taxation of foundation assets. One thing is certain: foundations, which don't have a lot of friends on the best of days, could be sitting ducks.

I'm almost certain that it was Jack Murrah, the former president of the Lyndhurst Foundation in Chattanooga, who first got me thinking about the fact that foundations have power. For more than a decade, my work at the Southeastern Council of Foundations was driven by the conviction that foundations could have a far greater impact upon the wellbeing of our region than they imagined. However, as I continued to promote this concept, I never described their opportunity as the use of power.

Foundations are uncomfortable with the notion that they might have power. They confuse it with the more conventional understanding of power as control or domination. But power can also include the humble willingness and sense of responsibility to recognize that significant resources can be applied to the solution of problems.

Not all of those resources are monetary. Because of their independence, foundations also have the power to convene partners around and focus attention upon major issues that virtually demand to be addressed. As Steve Gunderson, President of the Council on Foundations, put it to me, "At a time when the public sector is politically polarized and the private sector is focused on survival in a global economy, foundations may be the only institutions that can offer innovative, non-partisan leadership."

The Ultimate Challenge

As I was readying this book for publication, I had the opportunity to describe it to Rodney Jackson, President of the National Center for Black Philanthropy. In response, Rodney asked, "So, what do you think *is* the future of philanthropy?" I rambled on a bit about the points I just made in the preceding chapter. I also talked a bit about the need to promote all expressions of generosity, to inculcate the value of charitable behavior in young people, and to build stronger bridges between grant seekers and grant makers. Then, though, I heard myself saying, "I think the future of philanthropy will somehow be related to the way foundations respond to the widening gap between the rich and the poor."

Before you read further, please keep in mind that I remain adamant about the right of all foundations to disburse their grants in ways that reflect their sense of mission and/or the wishes of the donors whose wealth created them. Nonetheless, I also wish to share this concluding and highly personal reflection about foundations and their purpose.

The relationship between wealth and the needs of the poor is a topic that has preoccupied the attention of human beings for millennia. Among those who took a shot at sharing his thinking on the subject was Andrew Carnegie, the renowned industrialist and philanthropist. In 1889 he wrote something called "The Gospel of Wealth."

It's a fascinating treatise that could only have been written by a rich and somewhat patronizing man. Carnegie was not without wisdom. For example, he had great insight into the danger of very wealthy people ruining their children's lives by leaving them inheritances that would make it unnecessary for them to be productive citizens. This parsimonious Scotsman also deplored ostentatious spending and living on the part of the rich.

However, to his way of thinking it seems to be virtually ordained that some individuals are supposed to acquire great wealth, others are entitled to earn enough money to lead modestly comfortable lives and that the poor will always be with us. If you're a strict Calvinist, you may choose to conclude that this arrangement is proof of God's special favor for some folks. Or, if you're a liberation theologian, you might interpret this phenomenon as a call to bring about radical change. Whatever your perspective, when a company like Dell, the giant computer corporation in Texas, as I read a few years ago, could claim to have 1,400 millionaires on its payroll, and the incidence of hunger in Texas as well as throughout this country was rising, something's very wrong.

As a nation we are doing a lousy job of caring for the neediest of our people. A visitor from another planet could easily conclude, based upon our federal funding priorities, that we despise poor people, thoroughly dislike children and young people and, frankly, that we're not too crazy about our aging population—especially if they are poor.

Capitalism, despite its limitations, is an astonishing economic system and I am only one of millions who are the beneficiaries of the enormous wealth it has helped to create. Nonetheless, the evidence is clear that while those of us who are living comfortably continue to do even better, the poor are slipping further and further behind, and even the middle class is seeing most of its economic gains being eaten up by rising health care costs. The paradox of so much wealth and so much poverty in such close proximity to each other and the disappearance of a middle class should disturb all of us greatly. However, just as too many people for too long averted their eyes from the evil of legalized racial segregation, too many of us remain in deep denial about the enormous gap between the haves and have-nots—or, as one sardonic commentator put it, the growing divide between the rich and the really rich. In resigning ourselves to the seeming omnipresence of the poor (or justifying this toleration by citing Jesus or the Talmud), we neglect the fact that it is in the self-interest of many of us to ensure that the poor will indeed always be with us. Thus, for example, our flawed immigration policies tend to drive down the wages of the working poor, thereby making it possible for the rest of us to continue to enjoy amenities like landscaping services and affordable meals in restaurants.

To give him further due, Carnegie was truly convinced that his money carried with it the responsibility to use it on behalf of society. He especially favored the creation of institutions and facilities like libraries that would assist other Americans with ambition to pull themselves up by their own bootstraps. What Carnegie didn't take into account was that his kind of self-advancement is sometimes difficult to accomplish when you don't even own a pair of boots.

Bob Reich, an associate professor at Stanford University, wrote a provocative essay some time ago in which he asserted that philanthropy has failed in its responsibility to respond to the needs of the poor and the needy—a duty that he believes lies at the heart of its broad mission. Whether you believe that philanthropy has failed the poor, though, depends upon the lens through which you examine the issue.

Let me use the region in which I live as an example. Organized philanthropy is finally coming of age in the South. The numbers and assets of foundations have increased radically during the past 25 years and, at least from one perspective, the results are impressive. Our major universities and preparatory schools are flourishing; our cities are home to great arts centers and museums and botanical gardens and zoos. Atlanta can now boast of having the largest aquarium in the world. All of these achievements have been spurred by philanthropic wealth and generosity. Many of us in a South that was mired in poverty for a long time are experiencing a more comfortable and pleasant life as a result of philanthropy.

On the other hand, if you study the principal indicators of social wellbeing in our region, you would have to concede that philanthropy does not seem to have had a significant impact on the education of poor children or the provision of health care to them or their families. The Southern states chronically are at the bottom of all the national lists in these kinds of categories and have been there for many years.

Yet if you look more closely, it becomes clear that many philanthropic organizations have indeed made valiant efforts to direct their resources to support assistance to the neediest of the region's citizens. The "failure" of philanthropy, if we stick with Reich's indictment for a moment, is not a disinterest in poverty. It is too often an unwillingness to address its root causes.

It's not hard to identify individual examples of shiftless bums who really don't seem to have an interest in being employed. However, I've grown impatient with those tired old pronouncements about how the poor don't want to work. Most of the poor people I know want to be self-sufficient. They're just having a very difficult time trying to figure out how to do so on minimum wage rates that now purchase less than they did forty years ago.

It seemingly never occurred to Carnegie—or else he rejected the notion—that philanthropy might have a role to play in changing the policies and practices that keep people in poverty. Several years ago, Claire Gaudiani, the former president of Connecticut College, wrote a book called *The Greater Good*. In it she asserted that philanthropy can save the soul of capitalism. If she's correct, then foundations may have to do more than address the symptoms of poverty.

It's a pleasure to note that there are signs that the situation has changed somewhat during the course of the past several decades. Growing numbers of foundations have decided that they want their philanthropy to offer a hand up, not a handout. They are strategically using their grants to support job creation and job training and education in entrepreneurship and affordable housing and day care centers. All of these approaches and others like them strike me as appropriate examples of Maimonides' philanthropic priority of moving fellow human beings from a state of dependency to self-sufficiency.

Marty Strange, a longtime advocate for sustainable rural communities, doesn't need an essay to make the point far less cautiously than I have. As he asserted at a workshop that we convened a decade or so ago, "Philanthropy without justice is a sin."

The choice before all of us—for ethical and/or economic reasons and whether we operate in the private, not-for-profit, or governmental sectors—is this: will we continue to be satisfied with simply alleviating the needs of the poor and thereby fostering a condition of dependency, or will we advance liberty and opportunity for everyone by changing the policies and practices that help to make poverty the bane of the wealthiest country in the world.

EPILOGUE—THE BUSINESS OF HOPE

Lots of people are convinced that the world is going to hell. I think they do so because they see all of the rapid change that's occurring through the eyes of fear—a perspective that far too many of our political and religious leaders and radio shock jocks seem determined to encourage and exploit.

What sets apart much of the not-for-profit sector is that its practitioners see the world and embrace change through the eyes of hope. Nancy Neimann-Hoffman, a long-time friend, sent me a quote from Vaclav Havel, the former President of the Czech Republic. "Hope," he postulated, "is not prognostication; it is an orientation of the heart." Put another way, in our sector we choose to envision a world in which all its people are able to live in communities whose hallmarks are peace and justice, and we think it's worth patiently working toward that goal. The practice of hope, then, is not a vague yearning or passive dreaming. I feel enormously privileged to be working in the "hope business."

Throughout this book, I have suggested several directions in which I hope that this sector will move and identified characteristics that I hope it will embody. My greatest wish for the sector is that we all will demonstrate courageous leadership. To be sure, we must be law-abiding and ethically accountable; we need to exercise wise stewardship over the resources entrusted to us. In the final analysis, though, I believe that we're at the top of our game when we have the guts to take on tough challenges. We need to be ready to break ranks with our organizations' traditional guidelines, with our peers, and even with public opinion to tackle issues and problems from which it would have been much easier to avert our eyes.

Because we are human beings, our work will continue to be marked by good intentions but also riddled with inefficiencies. Crooks and charlatans will continue to appear in our ranks. They in turn will attract the scrutiny of lawmakers and the media, and we will periodically take new steps to reform ourselves further. We will be buffeted by rapidly changing demographic shifts and ever-accelerating technological revolutions. Common sense will sometimes seem in short supply, but we will keep muddling on. It all reminds me of the charter of St. Martin-in-the-Fields Church in London. Its concluding statement asserts: "We are committed to identifying and affirming what is good and identifying and opposing what is evil, and living as best we can in the mess in the middle."

David Brooks, writing recently in the New York *Times*, envisioned a modern Republican Party whose philosophy would emphasize "society as well as individuals, security as well as freedom, a social revival and not just an economic one and the community as opposed to the state." That's also pretty good summation of the kind of goals the not-for-profit sector embraces.

All in all, I believe the fundamental goodness of the sector will continue, and for that blessing we can all be deeply thankful. We exist not to reap a financial reward; our net gain comes from the pleasure of helping to repair and restore a world that can still dare to dream of becoming a beloved community.

Even as I'm completing this manuscript, we are experiencing a very disturbing economic recession. The value of foundation portfolios is shrinking, while not-for-profit organizations everywhere are nervously re-calculating budgets for the coming year and delaying the start of capital fund raising campaigns.

Is it, then, sheer idiocy to counsel folks—as I did in an earlier chapter—to see the world through the lens of abundance? I don't think so. As I have tried to contend, the work of the charitable sector involves far more than the preservation of endowments or the disbursal and use of grants for worthwhile purposes. Far worse than the shrinkage of financial assets would be the erosion of the spirit of generosity that's at the heart of what we do.

That spirit, I am confident, is not going to disappear. As it has during other difficult periods, the not-for-profit sector will again muster its reserves of creativity and courage to preserve the ideals of compassionate citizenship.

ABOUT THE AUTHOR

Martin Lehfeldt has spent the past 43 years working in or for the not-for-profit sector—a career that has included positions as a foundation program officer, a college development officer, the head of his own consulting firm, and the presidency of the Southeastern Council of Foundations (SECF). He also has been a volunteer board chair and board member of numerous not-for-profit organizations and was a facilitator and coordinator of two working groups for the Transatlantic Community Foundation Network.

His writing over the past four decades has included a wide variety of articles and columns, contributions to *An Agile Servant: Community Leadership by Community Foundations*; co-authorship of *The Sacred Call* (a biography of Donald L. Hollowell, civil rights attorney during the 1950s and 1960s), and editorship of and contributions to *On Our Way Rejoicing* (a collection of essays commemorating the 150th anniversary of Central Presbyterian Church in Atlanta. He also has written two plays and several hymn texts. Upon his retirement from SECF, the association published *Thinking about Things*, a compilation of his monthly columns from *Interchange*, the organization's newsletter.

Although retired from SECF, Lehfeldt continues to write, accept speaking engagements, and consult with not-for-profit organizations and grant-making foundations. He and his wife, Linda, live in Atlanta and have three productive mortgage-paying children and three grand-children.

Made in the USA
Lexington, KY
12 February 2010